My Home by the River

and Other Poems

By Mary E. Miller

Illustrated by E. Ruth Miller

There is a river, the streams whereof shall make glad the city of God, the holy place of the tabernacles of the most High. Psalm 46:4

Send correspondence to:

Cider Press Publications
P.O. Box 1101
Middlebury, IN 46540

Picture on front cover taken by Gloria Salavarria

Library of Congress Control Number (case bound version): 2008937645
Library of Congress Control Number (spiral bound version): 2008937597

ISBN Number (case bound version): 978-0-9821416-1-8
ISBN Number (spiral bound version): 978-0-9821416-0-1

Printed by Evangel Press
        2000 Evangel Way
        PO Box 189
        Nappanee, IN 46550

Foreword

By E. Ruth Miller

I am not sure when Mary, my youngest sister, began to notice poetry. She was in the second or third grade when she wrote her first poems. She hand printed them carefully onto tablet paper and threaded twisted yarn through a hole at the top to hold the sheets together.

Mary's first poem appears unedited as follows:

> School
> It is fun to go to school.
> In weather hot or cold or cool
> The sun may be shing brigt,
> Or a shade of lighen night.
>
> But if we are at any place
> I like to see a smiling face
> I do not like a frown so sad
> It is a smile that makes me glad.
>
> I would like everyone to be a friend
> My poam is coming to and end,
> 'Cause I don't know what to say
> And theres work to be done today.   M.E.M.

But the one I remember is the following (also unedited):

> Desaster
> Once upon a time
> long, long ago
> There were three sheep
> who had a wole buch of wool.
>
> One day one said
> Let us climb,
> To the very place
> The sun doth shine.

But it was so hot there, they bawled and they cried
but cried as the did the all fell and died.

Just think of the disaster of one littel thought,
Because the did listen, desather it brought. M.E.M.

The phrase, "They all fell and died," was quite surprising. We, her sisters, thought it was really too shocking, but Mary was pleased with her poems. And our mother was very encouraging.

When she was almost sixteen, she wrote the poem, "Poet's Troubles," which was later published in the *Young Companion* magazine. It reveals the frustration she was then feeling in writing poetry. She finished by expressing surprise at how the poem was turning out.

Poet's Troubles

I'd love to be a poet
 And write poems to thrill the heart--
Some poems to make my readers laugh
 Or make the teardrops start.
To stir the deep emotions
 To make them feel as I;
But it seems I cannot do it
 And I sometimes wonder why.

I cannot get the words to rhyme
 Exactly as they should.
And as to perfect rhythm
 At that I'm not so good.
It seems I simply cannot get
 In each and ev'ry line
The right amount of syllables
 To fit my poem's design.

Punctuation is another thing
 That often puzzles me
Where should I put the question marks?
 Where should the commas be?
There also is good grammar
 To give my skills a test
Sometimes "better" would fit better
 Where "best" would rhyme the best.

And when I've racked my tired brain
 To get it all "just so,"
I find I've missed another point!
 It's really quite a blow!
I've found the message that I'd meant
 To make my poem convey
Has somehow slipped elusively
 And gotten "clean away!"

Sometimes I'll put it in my drawer.
 Sometimes into the fire.
Somehow it doesn't sound as great
 As poets might desire.
Sometimes I think it's rather nice
 Although I seldom do.
All in all, it is enough
 To make a poet blue.

I'd better quit my ramblings
 Or this might turn to smoke.
This poem I might get printed;
 It's really quite a joke!
Although it isn't perfect
 This poem has proven me
To be a better poet
 Than I ever thought I'd be!

Seeing one of her poems in print for the first time encouraged her to write more.

As time went on, her poems continued to improve. Life's simple pleasures and experiences gave her a variety of subjects on which to write. Her propensity for reading and learning widened her horizons and enlarged her vocabulary. Some are delightfully humorous, some informative, and many are inspirational.

Mary works on her poems in her head while she goes about her work. She does not mind if we talk to each other while she is "poeming," but she asks us not to sing. Singing, she says, throws her poems out of rhythm.

Disappointments and her battles with cancer have deepened her faith in God which in turn have given her poems more depth. People are often touched by them. A cousin of ours gave a copy of "It Takes a Lot of Courage" to a man battling with cancer. He broke down and cried. "How does she know how it is?" he wondered. Our cousin answered, "Because she's been through it, too."

People have encouraged Mary to put her poems together in a book. We would reply, "We want to--someday." We thought we should wait until she had enough poems. But now "someday" is here, and we discovered she has more poems than we thought!

I have enjoyed working on this project with Mary. She has been very easy to please and most appreciative. We hope that you enjoy this book of poems.

By Mary E. Miller

When Ruthie was a little girl, she "just loved" to watch our father draw pictures or write in fancy script. How she admired these pieces of art! Often she would try to imitate the drawings and especially the fancy print. She didn't know then how useful her skill would be to her (and me) in illustrating this book.

I am grateful to Ruthie for all the hours she spent bent over the paper, using an ordinary ball point pen (or a felt-tip marker on a few occasions), dealing with streaks and blotches and pictures that just didn't look right. Practice has done much for her skill; the illustrations these days are done much more quickly than the first ones were. Just watching her, one would think drawing is easy!

Ruthie is responsible for more than just the illustrations. "For the Children" and a number of other poems were written at her suggestion. Many of the "How to's" were her idea. Early in our efforts to compile this book, I found myself letting Ruthie go ahead with many of the decisions about fonts, format, layout, etc. I was happy with the results and grateful to have someone else make those many little decisions. Thank you, Ruthie!

We also wish to thank the rest of the family for ALL the extra work they did so we could work on this book. We express our gratitude...

...To Mama who admired every poem and illustration.

...To Sam who gave his whole-hearted support.

...To Becky who proofread and proofread nearly every page.

...To Kathy who pushed this project forward and gets a lot of credit for the excerpts from the Christmas and diary entries. She willingly helped in many other ways.

Acknowledgments

We wish to express appreciation to all who have contributed to this book. We thank our many friends for their encouragement and for cheering us on. We give special acknowledgments to the following:

James L. Rogers whose kind and generous bequeathal covers the cost of printing this book.

Our dear friends who gave donations to help with the expenses of publishing the book.

Ruthie's kind employers who <u>encouraged</u> her to work on the book while on the job.

Our helpful friends who proofread so willingly.

Those who gave equipment (or money for equipment) which we used to prepare the manuscript.

Those who gave Ruthie pens which she used for illustrations.

Table of Contents

Chapter One

HOME AND FAMILY

The cider mill and house

My Home by the River

by Mary Elaine Miller

My riverside home is a wonderful place.
The stream to the west is the quiet mill race.
The one to the east with its livelier pace
    And its zig-zagging course is the river.

Our home has such wonderful places to play!
We laughed, and we sang, and we chattered away.
We quarreled, made up, and we grew day by day
    When we were but young by the river.

The years have moved onward since I was so small.
Young saplings have grown into trees broad and tall.
I like my old tree friends; I mourn when they fall,
    But change marks our home by the river.

Our grandparents left and are seen here no more.
Our father (blest parent!) has gone on before.
They left us with mem'ries, a wonderful store
    Of when they lived here by the river.

Our aunts and our uncles have come now and then.
Hard by here they grew into women and men.
Our cousins are happy to visit again
    The old Miller home by the river.

Our home has seen changes, but friends oft exclaim
In tones of nostalgia, "It still looks the same!"
"Like coming back home again," some of them claim,
    "To visit this place by the river."

The people who live here are special to me,
My mother (the dearest of mothers is she!),
One brother, three sisters, my dear family
    All live here at home by the river.

We sing, we converse, we laugh, and we weep.
The day is for toil and the night is for sleep.
We leave, but returning we're happy to keep
    Our home in the house by the river.

Some troubles perplex us, but blessings come, too.
We battle with illness, but health comes anew.
The clouds cast their shadows, but sunshine breaks through
    And touches our home by the river.

We struggle with weeds of the garden and heart.
We've nurtured fond dreams, and we've watched them depart,
But God gives us courage to make a new start,
    Each day in our home by the river.

God knoweth the future; we live day by day.
Perhaps new direction will shorten my stay.
If not, till death's angel shall call me away
    I'll live here at home by the river.

FATHER

Faithfully earning the clothing and bread

Assuming the role as the family's head

Taking the time to enjoy childish charms

Holding his children in strong, loving arms.

Employing, if needed, the use of the rod.

Raising his children to honor his God.

—MARY E. MILLER

Molding the lives that are under her care,

Over them drawing a blanket of prayer.

Though her extent of dominion is small,

Here she is queen and servant of all!

Ever perceiving the good in each one,

Rich is her love for each daughter and son.

— MARY E. MILLER

Our Family

This is an introduction to our family. First we must tell you about our parents.

Vernon E. Miller, whom we call "Papa," was born in 1932, in the house at the end of our lane. He was the youngest of thirteen children and was raised in the Amish-Mennonite faith.

In 1950, he helped his father and brothers build the house where we now live, and he moved here with his parents. By this time all of his older siblings that had grown to adulthood were married.

Alta I. Marks "Mama" was born near Union, Michigan, the youngest of 5 children. She became an R.N. at Swedish Covenant Hospital in Chicago.

In 1956, Papa's father was hospitalized with head injuries. Papa would stay with him at nights. Our mother was working at the hospital, and that is where they met. After *much* prayerful consideration they were married in 1959, our mother agreeing to join the Mennonite church.

Growing up in the country, Mama knew how to milk a cow and tend the chickens. She would even help her father on his carpenter jobs. Still, her mother said she was not ready for marriage until she knew how to butcher a chicken. So before she and Papa were married, she had to kill a couple of chickens. Happily for Mama, after they were married, Papa did that part of the butchering process!

Mama was not so sure about quitting her job as a nurse to stay at home when we children came along. But she did, and she never wanted to punch a time clock again.

In 1964, our parents bought a piece of land from Grandma Miller out by the road. There Papa built a house for his wife and son, and that is where we four daughters joined the family. He was a wonderful father. He spent a lot of time with us, teaching us our responsibility to a loving God and to appreciate the simple things of life. He enjoyed reading aloud to us from a good storybook at bedtime, even after we were grown. Then we would kneel for bedtime prayers, and he would ask God to send His guardian angels to watch over us.

In 1976, our parents sold the house by the road, and we moved to where we now live. Grandma Miller had moved in with us (up by the road) so we could care for her. Now she was home again in the house by the river. Before long our mother's parents moved into a mobile home beside us so we could care for them as well.

Papa quit his job as a plumber to work at home in the cider mill. The business went well, and in the summer he would usually make some improvement in the mill. During the height of the season, we would sometimes have a line of customers waiting for opening time at 7:OO A.M. But no matter how long the line, Papa took time for family devotions. He said his business was raising his family.

Papa was a collector and a historian. He especially was interested in area history and memorabilia and railroad artifacts. He tried not to spend much money on his collection and delighted in making something out of what most people would throw away.

A classic example of this was a car horn he bought at a garage sale for $5.00. The bulb that you squeezed to make the air was cracked and had leaks in it. A new bulb for $75.00 was too much money. Then when he had his heart surgery in 2003, he wanted to bring home his ambu bag instead of having it thrown away. He hooked that bulb up to the horn and set it up with his collection in the boiler room. People got a chuckle out of it, especially his cardiologist!

Papa often visited the sick and the elderly. He would sometimes want all of us to go with him, and he would have us sing for them. He liked to pass out extra garden produce and yellow delicious apples to area folks. During his last sickness he was hoping to get better because he wanted to spend even more time visiting. He passed away in 2004, at the age of 72.

Mama says her work is her hobby. She does not figure her labor to show that buying prepared food would be more cost effective. She gladly *gives* her time and labor to her family. She believes in getting up early because, she says, those are the golden hours. She also believes in sitting down to three balanced meals a day. It is a wonderful thing to come into the house and know that your mother is there, cheerfully trying to keep everything running smoothly.

Samuel A. Miller "Sam" is the oldest and only brother. He is kept busy with the business and the upkeep of the place. He enjoys mechanical work, and he keeps our vehicles in running order. He sometimes gets overwhelmed with all the work but tries to be optimistic. Awhile back someone asked him how it was going, and he cheerfully replied, "Well, I am managing to keep up with the interruptions!"

Sam likes to read and keeps reading material handy for spare moments. He explains current and historical events to his sisters. Sam likes to watch the sky. He is one that "never misses a sunset." When he was younger, he memorized a number of lengthy poems. As a young girl, Mary listened with admiration to his recitations which deepened her growing interest in poetry.

Rebecca I. Miller "Becky" has become everyone's helper. She helps Sam with his work when a second person is needed. She does chores for Mary when Mary does not feel up to doing them. She mows grass for Ruthie when Ruthie is too busy elsewhere. She helps Kathy with her job as caregiver for an elderly couple in our neighborhood so Kathy can have more time at home. Then she hurries into the kitchen to help Mama get the meal on the table.

While all of us help in the garden, it is Becky who is the gardener at heart. She starts the plants in the little greenhouse. She likes to find the first ripe strawberries, the first asparagus spike, and other produce as it begins to ripen.

E. Ruth Miller "Ruthie" is very much at home in the sick room.   She helps care for the elderly in their homes and finds this work rewarding. She was grateful for all her previous experience when Papa was sick, but she realizes there is always more to learn!

Ruthie also enjoys children. If visiting children need to be entertained, she soon has them happily playing with her.

Kathleen J. Miller "Kathy" is our salesperson. She enjoys the work in the mill. She willingly drops her work or leaves the dinner table to take care of a customer. She is eager to see which of her customer friends has come or to meet a new one.

Kathy is very good at remembering the customers' names and details from previous visits. Sometimes this puts us, her sisters, in a quandary. Because of the family resemblance, the customers take us for her, and they are disappointed when we do not recognize them.

Kathy follows our mother's example of keeping in touch with many of our friends.

Mary E. Miller, born in 1972, is the youngest in the family. She loves it when she feels good and can do whatever she does with vigor and vim. Papa would comment, "She is the merriest of them all!"

Mary likes to work outside with the animals. When she was very young, someone asked her, "Are you 'Mary, Mary quite contrary'?" and she replied, "No, I'm the Mary that had the little lamb!" And she did have a pet lamb at the time.

Mary enjoys helping Sam cut wood or with repair or building jobs. She thinks it is great fun to till the garden. She likes to pick wild raspberries and go for long walks in the woods. It is hard for her when she has to stay out of the sun because of her treatments.

But she also likes to work in the kitchen with Mama, and Mama likes to have her efficient, enthusiastic help. The two of them can plan and cook and bake up a storm. Mary gets up early to stir up a large batch of bread dough on bread-making day. Mary tries to see to it that no food goes to waste so we never know what leftover food she might sneak into the main dish. But as long as it tastes good, I guess we should not complain, should we?

Mary likes to knit and crochet and has made a number of articles, especially mittens.

Mary also enjoys memorizing poems and scripture verses. She tries to remember where various scriptures are found. This has come in handy when writing some of her poems.

We are members of a small Mennonite (conservative) church where Papa was a minister. He often used everyday examples to illustrate a spiritual truth, and Mary frequently finds herself using this same technique in her poems.

Our aim in life is to ever walk closer to the Lord, following His holy will. We know of a surety that this is the best path to follow. Proverbs 4:18 describes this beautiful path so well, "But the path of the just is as the shining light, that shineth more and more unto the perfect day." God help us to remain faithful!

Our Debt to Our Parents

--Mary Elaine Miller

We owe to you, our parents dear,
   A debt of such degree
That it defies all measurement.
For us, your children, you have spent
   Yourselves unstintingly.

How well we know we never can
   Begin to pay it all,
That principle, consisting of
Your tender care and thoughtful love
   Since we were young and small.

But interest payments can be made,
   Those payments always due,
By giving you our warm respect.
Your tender love we shall reflect,
   Returning it to you.

But never fear that we shall chafe
   Beneath that duty's weight,
Or dread those payments thus to meet,
For love has made those duties sweet,
   And love's glad strength is great.

And when we fail to measure up
   To all of our ideal;
When overcome with busyness,
When moments of forgetfulness,
   Our humanness reveal,

We know your love holds firmly still
   Your patience still endures.
We trust this love will never cease
But ever year by year increase
   To bless our lives and yours.

A Father's Love

--Mary E. Miller

How great the abundance of fatherly love
　He showered upon us each day!
How tearfully sad to reflect on the thought
　That he has been taken away.

The many fine qualities marking his life
　We lovingly, slowly review.
We knew all along he possessed them, but now
　How brightly their value shines through!

His love oft constrained him to discipline us.
　He always desired our good.
Our small childish problems, our growing-up fears
　His fatherly heart understood.

He strove to stand firmly, if need be, alone.
　His aim was to always do right.
To watch o'er his children, to guard us with prayer
　Was always his care and delight.

He loved to provide us with ev'ry good thing,
　Our food, shelter, clothes, and much more.
But now, without Papa, our lives will be changed
　And never the same as before.

Do memories only remain with us now,
　Those mem'ries so precious and dear?
Ah, no, for our Heavenly Father abides.
　His Presence will always be near.

God is the best Father in earth or in heav'n.
　His love is unmeasured and strong.
He disciplines us for the sake of our good
　To keep us from ruin and wrong.

He has for His children a pitying heart.
　He listens to every pray'r.
His wisdom and character always are right.
　He watches our souls with great care.

His bounty provides us with ev'ry good thing
　His wisdom declares to be best.
His comforting promises surely declare
　His children are richly well blessed.

Oh, Papa, how many examples you leave
　Adorning the pathway you trod!
How thankful we are that you taught us to know
　Our Heavenly Father, our God!

This poem was read at our father's funeral, November 2004.

I have no greater joy than to hear that my children walk in truth. III John 4

The Best Tribute

What is the best tribute to give to our parents

As thanks for the love and the care they have given?

"Not roses or presents or praises, dear children,

But to follow our steps on the pathway to heaven."

M.E.M.

FOR THE CHILDREN

Simple Toys

--Mary E. Miller

Often the simple and near-at-hand things--
Buttons and boxes and blankets and strings--
Make inexpensive and wonderful toys,
Delighting young maidens and thrilling the boys.

How to Make Connected Cutouts:
Using a piece of paper (it can be a newspaper) fold it back and forth across its length. Fold the paper like a fan, making sure the folds on both sides are even with each other.
Draw an outline of an object on the top layer. Bring at least one point on each side out to the fold. Cut it out, leaving the points on the fold intact so that when you unfold it, your object will be connected.

Find a big box (you might ask at a store),
And (please do be careful!) cut windows and door.
What a fine playhouse! A great place to hide!
A den, if you'd rather. Just come crawl inside.

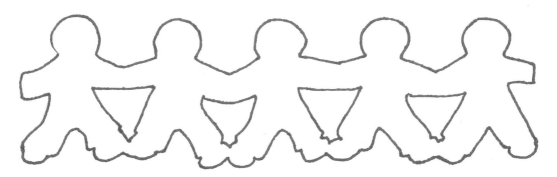

If there is a clothes line strung up in your yard,
Making a tent is not really so hard.
Sev'ral old blankets pinned well to the line,
Spread out and weighted will suit you just fine.

A giant-sized button, a string, long and stout,
Put them together and twirl them about.
Pull, now relax, now pull it again.
Dizzy old button. Just watch that thing spin!

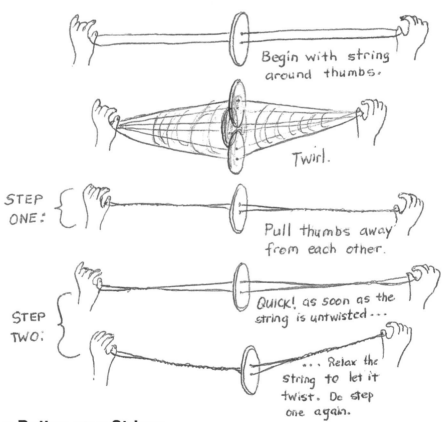

Begin with string around thumbs.

Twirl.

STEP ONE: Pull thumbs away from each other.

STEP TWO: Quick! as soon as the string is untwisted... ...Relax the string to let it twist. Do step one again.

How to Spin a Button on a String:
Take a piece of stout string such as #10 crochet thread or kite string about 50 inches long.
Thread it in and out of the two holes in a large button. Knot the ends of the string together.
Hold the loops of both ends of the string over your thumbs with the button in the center.
Twirl the button around and around until the string is twisted.
Step 1. Pull your thumbs away from each other, unwinding the string.
Step 2. *Quick!* as soon as the string becomes untwisted, move your thumbs closer together so that the string twists again. When it is twisted, do step 1 again.
Do step 1 and step 2 over and over to keep your button spinning. At first it may be hard to keep it going, but it is easy once you get the feel of it.

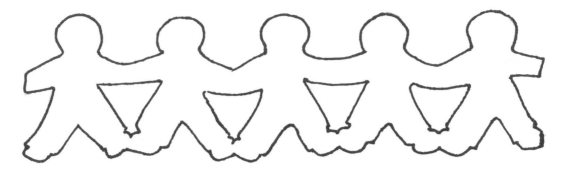

A pencil, a pin, and a paper that's square.
Cut it and fold it and pin it with care.
Blow it or move it and watch it go 'round,
Making a fluttery, papery sound.

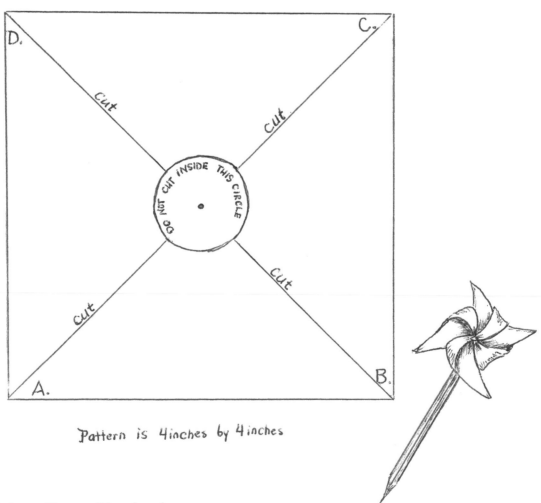

Pattern is 4inches by 4inches

How to Make a Paper Pinwheel:

Cut out a square of paper following the pattern. Cut along the lines. Bring points A, B, C, and D to the center, and pin them together with a straight pin. Poke the pin through the center of the pinwheel. Poke the pin into the side of a pencil eraser without bending the pin. Do not flatten the pinwheel. Pull the points against the pinhead and push the center of the pinwheel against the eraser. Blow into the pinwheel or wave it in the air to make it spin.

Read the directions. Put water to boil.
Get out the flour, salt, alum, and oil.
Mix all together. Add coloring, too.
What a nice ball of playdough for you!

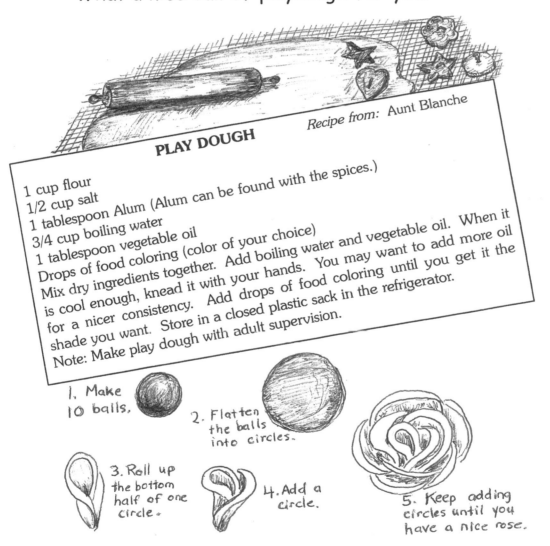

PLAY DOUGH   Recipe from: Aunt Blanche

1 cup flour
1/2 cup salt
1 tablespoon Alum (Alum can be found with the spices.)
3/4 cup boiling water
1 tablespoon vegetable oil
Drops of food coloring (color of your choice)
Mix dry ingredients together. Add boiling water and vegetable oil. When it is cool enough, knead it with your hands. You may want to add more oil for a nicer consistency. Add drops of food coloring until you get it the shade you want. Store in a closed plastic sack in the refrigerator.
Note: Make play dough with adult supervision.

1. Make 10 balls.

2. Flatten the balls into circles.

3. Roll up the bottom half of one circle.

4. Add a circle.

5. Keep adding circles until you have a nice rose.

How to Make a Rose Out of Play Dough:
Make 10 little balls the size of a marble out of play dough. Flatten each into a round circle. Roll up the bottom half of one of the circles. Using that for the center of the rose, keep adding the other circles to make a nice rose. You may not need all of the circles.

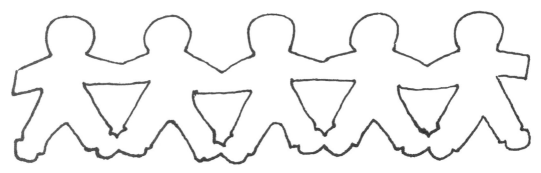

Fold up a paper in half and then
Cut it and cut it again and again.
Unfold it and fasten the edges with glue
And there is a lantern of paper for you.
But wait! Do NOT run for the matches, my friend.
It isn't a real one, it's only pretend.

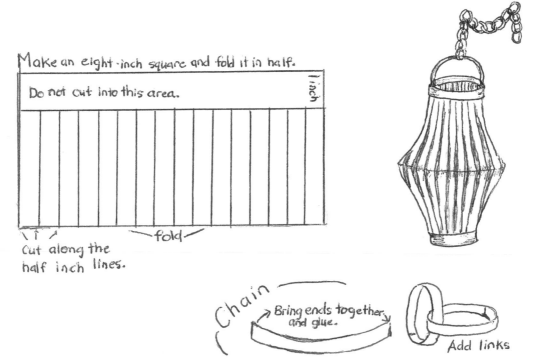

Make an eight-inch square and fold it in half.

Do not cut into this area.

1 inch

fold

Cut along the
half inch lines.

Chain

Bring ends together
and glue.

Add links

How to Make a Paper Lantern:

Use a paper 8 by 8 inches. You may wish to color the paper or use construction paper.
Fold the paper in half. Mark off a 1 inch line across the top. Do not cut past this line.
Beginning at the one side, draw a line every 1/2 inch all the way across. Leaving it folded,
cut each line.
Unfold the lantern and make it round by connecting both sides. Glue the sides together. Cut
a 1/2 by 6 inch strip and paste it on for the handle.
You can make a chain by cutting 1/2 by 4 inch strips. Glue the ends of a strip together to
make a link. Put another strip through the loop and glue its ends together for the second
link. Keep adding links to make the chain as long as you wish. Attach it to the lantern's
handle. You may want to hang this in your room for a decoration or give it to your grandma.

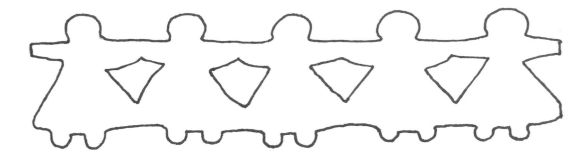

Lay out a hanky all nice and flat.
Fold it and roll it this way and that.
Now it's a hammock, and there in its nest
Little twin babies are taking their rest.

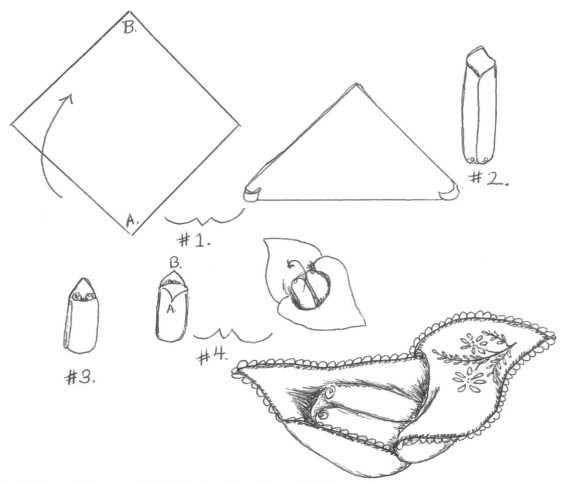

How to Make a Hammock Out of a Handkerchief:
1. Lay a handkerchief out flat. Bring point A. up to point B. to make a triangle.
2. Roll both bottom points toward each other until they meet right in the center.
3. Bring up the bottom of the two rolls, folding them in half.
4. Hold the rolls in place while separating points A. and B. Keep holding on to the rolls while pulling point A. away from point B. The rolls will become half the size. These are the twin babies. Tuck them snugly down into the hammock.
Hold point A. with one hand and point B. with the other, swinging them back and forth.

Look at this bottle I'm showing to you.
Once it held lotion or maybe shampoo.
(I guess you are young with a heart good and stout.)
Eeeek! What was that? It's a string flying out!
This is a trick that is soon overdone,
But once in a while it really is fun.

How to Make a Surprise in a Bottle:
Take an empty lotion bottle that has a small opening with a cap that snaps shut. Cut a heavy string such as #10 crochet thread or the string from a bird seed bag 20 or so inches long. Knot one end several times to make a knot larger than the hole in the cap. Put the knotted end into the bottle and thread the other end through the small hole in the cap. Screw on the cap and tie another large knot on the end of the string that is outside the bottle. Have all of the string inside the bottle with only the knot outside. Show it to a friend who can handle a surprise. While your friend is looking at it, give the bottle a hard, quick squeeze, and the string will fly out. Be careful not to do it right in your friend's face.

Where can a cradle for Dolly be found?
Take an old salt box that's empty and round.
Cut out the middle with caution and care.
Cover with beautiful paper. Now there!
Find a small pillow that's comfy and deep.
Rock-a-bye, rock-a-bye, Dolly's asleep.

How to Make a Cradle Out of a Round Salt Box:
Take an empty, round salt (or oatmeal) box. Carefully cut a large rectangle out of the middle. Cover the box with pretty paper such as wrapping paper. Glue it down smoothly and well.
If you cannot find a pillow to fit your cradle, simply fold up a doll blanket or a square of cloth to make a soft bed for your doll.
If you do not have a doll to fit inside, follow the directions below on how to make a handkerchief doll.

How to Make a Handkerchief Doll:
1. Lay the cloth handkerchief out flat.
2. Roll up both sides until they meet right in the middle.
3. Fold the top down at least half of the way.
4. Turn the doll around and single knot the rolled up sides over the front of the doll. Pull on the ends to stretch them out a bit. These are the arms.
5. Tug out the bottom of the rolls a bit for the feet. Arrange the head to make it rounder and fluff out the skirt.

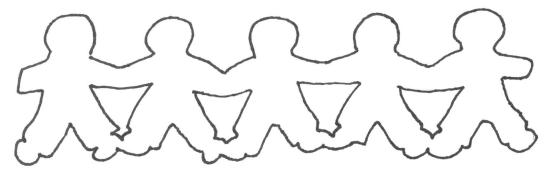

Here's how the simple grass whistle is made.
Look at the grasses and find a long blade.
Tuck it between your two thumbs now--just so.
Stretch it out tightly and blow (squawk!), and blow!

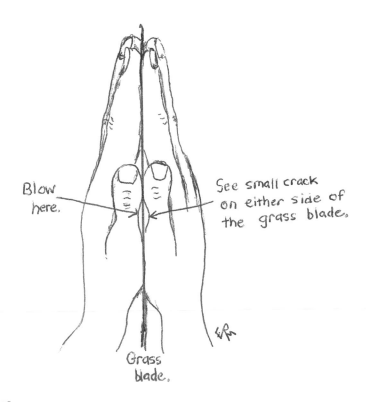

Blow here.

See small crack on either side of the grass blade.

Grass blade.

How to Make a Grass Whistle:

Pick a blade of grass at least 5 inches long and not more than 1/4 inch wide. (You may need to tear the blade lengthwise to make it more narrow.) Use a strong grass, such as quack grass. Put your hands flat together and then make your thumbnails face you. Your palms will move away from each other a little, making an airway.

Tuck the blade of grass between your thumbs. Make the blade taut. Put your lips up against your thumbs between the two top joints and blow.

This will probably take some practice. You may be blowing too hard or not hard enough. Make sure your hands are in the right position. Check that your grass blade is held tightly enough so that there is a tiny crack on either side of it between the thumb joints.

Once you get good at it, you can whistle with almost any piece of grass. You may also be able to squawk out a little tune on it by stretching the blade tighter and relaxing it for the different pitches.

For those who find projects like these to be fun,
The list of excitement has only begun.
Active young minds that lift up their wings
Can find great adventures with ev'ryday things.

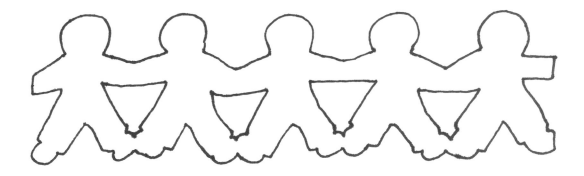

Dear Children,

We hope you enjoy this section which we made especially for you. If you have trouble figuring out any of the directions, ask your grandparents if they learned how to do them when they were young.

It is true that if you like this kind of projects, the list of excitement has only begun. Do not think that you have to have expensive toys to have fun. Often the simple things make you use your imagination more.

When we were small, we enjoyed these toys. When we played in our clothes line tent, we liked to cook meals in a plastic bucket over a pretend fire. We would gather leaves and wild flowers and add them to cold water to make soup. Daisies made great-looking eggs with their white petals around a yellow center. Even though we had toy dishes, it was more fun to gather large leaves for make-believe dishes and twigs for the utensils.

Helping with the work can even be fun if you use your imagination. We would sometimes write out cleaning jobs on slips of paper and then race to see who could do the most jobs. Sometimes we would play "garbage man" and collect the toys and clutter until we had the doll buggy filled. Then we would dash around putting our collection of things away. Then we were ready for the next load.

Sometimes we would take turns by rooms pretending one was the king and the rest were servants. The king would stand in one place with a yardstick, ordering the servants around, "Ruthie, clear off the bed!" and, "Kathy, line up the shoes!" etc. We did not mind being ordered around because we knew our turn to be the king would come. (By the way, the yardstick was only to wave in the direction of the work and NOT to beat the servants!)

If you do not have a brother or sister close to your age to help you play, you might have to use your imagination even more. Our mother was 8 years younger than the brother next to her. She often played alone. When she would play a game such as checkers, she would take a turn with her right hand. Then her left hand would take a turn.

Our imagination can be used for good and beautiful things or for mean and ugly things. We are happiest when we choose the good and beautiful.

Your Friends,
The Miller Family

Our Mother's Reply

There were dishes to do when we were but small,
    My three older sisters and I.
Of course, we didn't like to (what little girl does?)
    And so we would grumble and sigh.
"Oh, Mom, do we have to?" we'd ask with a groan
    In a rather undaughterly way.
And Mama would answer in calm, cheerful tones,
    "No, not if you **want** to," she'd say.

"Oh, yes, then we **want** to!" What bright, eager smiles!
    (Before we had quite learned the trick.)
"Then do them," our logical mother would say,
    Her answer was ready and quick.
And, oh, then the feeling of hopeless despair
    To know we were cleverly caught.
But now, some years after, we grant she was right
    And value the lesson she taught.

--Mary E. Miller

Excerpts from our Diary and Christmas Letters

October 23, 1991--Wednesday: Do you know how hard it is to keep ahead of one's mother? It seems every time we do something for Mama she thinks of something else to do, but this morning we did have her stumped for a bit. When Mama said that she could knead the bread dough, Kathy offered, "I'll knead it." "Well," Mama said, "I'll wash the breakfast dishes," but Ruthie told her she would. So Mama thought she'd go look after Grandma, but Mary said she was planning to do that. Then Mama said she could jug the 2 gallons of cider and we told her, "No, Becky is going to do that." And for once Mama wondered (for just a bit) what she would do!

January 28, 1993--Thursday: If our family can not be on time, it is not because we lack clocks. Papa recently refinished a clock which he was given years ago. It was in pieces when he received it. Now in our dining room, living room, and kitchen we have 5 clocks with pendulums, four of which strike on the hour and half-hour. There are also two in the bedrooms.

Christmas letter, 1993: You can't accuse Mama of being unfriendly. One day she waved at someone, and when she looked closer, she saw it was a scarecrow.

June 14, 1994--Tuesday: This evening we made ice cream in the hand-crank freezer, but it tasted awful. We put salt on the ice to make it colder, and the salt water leaked through a hole in the canister. None of us thought we could handle more than a taste--and hardly that. Papa fixed the hole, and then we made orange-pineapple sherbet--delicious!

August 21, 1996--Wednesday: When Papa went out at 5:00 A.M., he was surprised how well he could see the boat. It had not rained much here, but it had rained quite a bit elsewhere, making the millrace quite high. He took out 6 flood gates.

October 30, 1996--Wednesday: Mary and Andy, a boy we babysit, cooked vegetable soup back in the pasture on an open fire. While they were back there, they saw the sheep run and then discovered a fox which came quite close to them. Sam had seen one last week. Andy likes to cook like the pioneers did. He and Mary have even tried baking bread and cookies but they tended to burn a little. However, the soup is really good.

April 18, 1997--Friday: This evening Sam helped Andy measure the rate of water flow over the dam. They figured it at 400 gallons per second.

April 28, 1998--Tuesday: We were given a lot of edible soy beans which are good to a point, but we wonder how to use them all. Usually we just fix them like baked navy beans, but Mary has become quite ingenious in the matter. We never know where her "ground up beans" will turn up. One meal they were in the casserole and in the apple pie. Today she put them into her batch of bread. Everything has turned out surprisingly well, but we just hope she doesn't add them to our drinking water yet!

Christmas letter, 2000: Mary recently dreamed that she was writing a poem. It went something like this:

When you wake up in the morning
    At 3 o'clock at dawn,
You wonder where the buttercups
    And dandelions have gone.

August 22, 2002--Thursday: Today is Papa and Mama's 43rd wedding anniversary. After we milked the cow a little early this evening, we left for Marshall, MI. We had our supper on trays and ate on the way. (In the mid-forties Papa's family lived near Marshall for about a year. Papa remembered the fountain in Marshall and thought it would be a nice place to visit.) We arrived at the fountain about dark. The lights were soon lit, and they were constantly changing from white to blue, then to green, yellow, red, and then back to white. It was pretty and fascinating. We had a pleasant evening.

Christmas letter, 2005: In May, Mary decided to replace the wooden shingles on the old milkhouse where we keep garden tools. It was surprising who all helped her with advice. Years ago Mama and Aunt Esther had reshingled a small roof, and Mama remembered how to do it. Sam and Andy gave advice, and Uncle Glenn explained how to offset the cracks. Even her doctor spent time discussing how to put on wooden shingles when Mary was in for a check up.
    We other girls helped Mary tear off the 80 square feet of shingles. We lined up and nailed on the new ones, row by row. Sam helped replace some of the rotten under boards, and he put on the ridge cap.

August 29, 2006--Tuesday: Recently while Sam was mowing, his straw hat was knocked off by a trumpet vine, and he mowed right over it. The poor hat looks like it belongs on a scarecrow.

January 22, 2008--Tuesday: Mary was lamenting the fact that she just did not get much done today. Mama asked her, "What were you doing at 5:00 this morning when you stirred up the bread dough? Just *loafing* around?"

WHO IS IT?

We have washed the dirty dishes,
  And their sadness now appears.
They are waiting in the drainer
  Well bedewed with shiny tears.

If the one who holds the dishtowel
  Takes her time and uses care,
She will amply be rewarded
  By the smiles the dishes wear.

But when I am in a hurry
  As so often is the case,
I confess I leave some teardrops
  On each sad, reproachful face.

I'm so glad I have a servant,
  Who does splendid work for me.
He is always very helpful,
  And he doesn't charge a fee.

I'd be lost, I fear, without him.
  He is Johnny-on-the-spot,
For he comes without my bidding
  If I think of him or not.

Don't you think he's full of pity?
  When my dishes start to cry,
With his gentle breath he comforts
  Ev'ry dish until it's dry.

I suppose you've used him often.
  He can boast of world-wide fame.
Yes, that's right! Evaporation
  Is my helpful servant's name.

                    —Mary Miller

28

A Good Cook

She is a good cook
Who can look through a book
    To find recipes new and exciting,
Who goes to the store
If she needs something more
    To make that new dish so inviting.

But...

She who does not demand
More than just what's on hand,
    Who does not all those extras desire,
Yet can stir up a dish
To fulfill ev'ry wish
    Is the kind of good cook I admire!

M.E.M.

Recipe for
Crow's Nest Pudding

Plain Cake

1 cup sugar	1 cup milk
1/4 cup shortening	2 cups flour
1 teaspoon vanilla	3 teaspoons baking powder
1 beaten egg	1/2 teaspoon salt

Cream sugar and shortening together; beat in eggs and vanilla. Add sifted dry ingredients alternately with milk.

Blueberries

4 cups blueberries	4 tablespoons minute tapioca
1/2 to 1 cup brown sugar	2 cups water

Grease two 2"x8"x8" glass baking pans and put half of the blueberries, sugar, tapioca, and water into each. Stir gently. Pour half of plain cake batter over the blueberries in each pan. Bake at 350° until toothpick inserted in center of cake comes out clean. Serve warm or cold with milk or ice cream.

Variation: Substitute peaches, raspberries, cherries, or other suitable fruits for the blueberries. You may want to change the name of the pudding to fit the color. Suggestions: Oriole's Nest or Cardinal's Nest Pudding.

Sugar Cookies

1 cup shortening	5 cups sifted flour
2 cups white sugar	3 teaspoons baking powder
3 eggs, well beaten	1 teaspoon salt
1 teaspoon vanilla	1/2 teaspoon soda
1 cup sour milk or buttermilk	

Cream shortening and sugar; beat in eggs and vanilla. Add sour milk alternately with dry ingredients.
Drop dough by rounded teaspoonfuls onto cookie sheet. Bake at 350° for 15 minutes, or until bottom of cookie is slightly browned. Remove from cookie sheet and frost while still hot. Makes about 4 to 5 dozen cookies.

Frosting

4 cups powdered sugar	About 3 tablespoons milk
1/3 cup butter or margarine, softened	1 teaspoon vanilla

Beat together powdered sugar, butter, vanilla, and 2 tablespoons milk. Continue to beat while slowly adding enough milk to make the frosting just thin enough to spread easily.

Recipe for

Easy Chocolate Cake

3 cups flour
2 cups sugar
2 teaspoons soda
6 tablespoons cocoa
1 teaspoon salt
2 teaspoons vanilla
2 tablespoons vinegar
3/4 cup vegetable oil or melted shortening or butter
2 cups cold water

Sift dry ingredients together. Add most of the water and stir thoroughly. Add rest of water and other ingredients and stir again. Line the bottom of a 9"x13" cake pan with waxed paper. Grease pan and paper. Pour batter into prepared pan and bake at 350° until toothpick inserted in center comes out clean.

We learned to bake when we were quite small. Our mother taught us to mix the shortening and sugar, add the eggs (which needed to be beaten well), and the flavoring. Everything needed to be mixed well and the flour sifted for a light cake. One day we three oldest girls saw Mary stirring up this cake, and we were shocked to see how she did it. We tried to tell her that was not how to stir up a cake. She calmly kept on mixing the cake. Later when our mother heard about it, she said Mary was right. Mary had learned to use this recipe while we others were in school.
E. Ruth Miller

Pie Crust

6 cups flour
3 teaspoons baking powder
1 teaspoon salt
2 cups vegetable shortening
1 beaten egg with enough cold water to make 1 cup

Sift dry ingredients together. Cut shortening into flour with pastry cutter or rub between hands until it is crumbly. Add egg and water a little at a time, mixing lightly. Add a little more water if needed. Gather dough together and shape into six or seven balls. Roll out dough and fit into pie pans. This will make 6 or 7 single pie crusts. Extra crusts can be frozen. Before baking an empty pie shell, poke with a fork a number of times on sides and bottom.
You may want to use the leftovers to make one or two extra crusts for tops. Anything left over after that can be made into Lady Fingers. Place a spoonful of apple butter on a scrap of dough perhaps 2"x3". Roll it up and place on greased glass baking pan. Bake.
Or you can make "crackers" by placing small scraps of rolled-out dough onto cookie sheet or pie pan. Sprinkle with seasoned salt or cinnamon and sugar. Keep a close eye on these when you bake them because it is easy to let them get too brown.

Recipe for
Raspberry Cream Pie

(Amounts for 8-inch pie in parenthesis)

Pastry for 9-inch pie, unbaked (8-inch)
1 1/2 cups sugar (1 cup)
3/4 cup flour (1/2 cup)
1/8 teaspoon salt (pinch)
2 cups cream (1 1/2 cups)
2 cups fresh or frozen black raspberries (1 1/2 cups)

Sift dry ingredients together. Slowly stir in cream. Place raspberries in pie shell and pour cream mixture into shell. Carefully set into preheated oven (350°). To test for doneness, give pie a quick little shake. Pie is done when center is firm.
To shorten baking time, heat 1 1/2 cups of cream in sauce pan on stove until hot. Mix dry ingredients with the remaining 1/2 cup cream and stir until smooth. Stir in hot cream. Proceed with recipe.
Great-grandma Holdeman made raspberry cream pies and so did her daughter, our Grandma Marks. Uncle Don would tell how he would find "a handful of raspberries" when he was a boy. He would take them to Grandma Marks, and she would bake a pie with them.
Usually my mother and I bake raspberry pies for the Holdeman Reunion. One time perhaps ten years ago we made strawberry pie. One of the cousins said, "Always save room for ..." She looked around and finished lamely, "...strawberry pie, I guess." Since then we've stuck with the raspberry pies!
Mary E. Miller

Raisin Filled Cookies

In the latter thirties
  Grandma Wilma took
Home Extension classes
  to better learn to cook.
And one day the leader
  said to all the class,
"You may well forget me
  while the long years pass.
But I have a recipe
  which will stick with you."
(Well, the last prediction
  certainly came true!)
Then in nineteen forty,
  the year before she died,
Joy gave each a Christmas box,
  and they found inside
Yummy, yummy cookies
  which were raisin filled.
Alta well remembers
  that she was so thrilled!
Grandma Wilma made them
  through the passing years.
What was more delightful
  than these treats of hers?
Now no Marks reunion
  ever seems complete
If there are no cookies,
  raisin-filled, to eat.
Home Extension Leader,
  what you said was true.
We still have the recipe,
  many thanks to you!   M.E.M.

Recipe for
Raisin Filled Cookies

Dough
1 cup white sugar
1 cup brown sugar
1 cup butter or other shortening
3 eggs, well beaten
1 teaspoon vanilla
1/3 cup sour milk or buttermilk
5 cups all-purpose flour
1 teaspoon soda
1 teaspoon baking powder

Cream shortening and sugars together; beat in eggs and vanilla. Add milk alternately with sifted dry ingredients. Refrigerate several hours or overnight.

Divide dough into portions. Roll about 1/8 inch thick. Cut with large round cookie cutter and place on cookie sheet. Place a spoonful of raisin filling on the cookie, spreading it evenly, but keeping it away from the edges. Place another cookie on top and press edges together. Sprinkle sugar on top. Bake at 350° until lightly browned.

Filling

1 1/4 cups ground raisins (use meat grinder)*
1 1/4 cups water
1 cup white sugar
2 1/2 level tablespoons all-purpose flour
1 1/4 teaspoons vanilla

Heat raisins and water together over low to medium heat. Stir flour and sugar together and add to boiling raisin mixture. Return to boil, stirring constantly and being careful not to let the hot mixture splash you. Remove from heat and stir in vanilla.

*Instead of grinding raisins in meat grinder, you can boil 2 cups whole raisins with the water. After they are nicely plumped (5 to 10 minutes), chop in blender.

My Treasure Chest

--Mary Elaine Miller

In my treasure chest of mem'ries
    Lies many a precious gem.
And stories of grandparents
    I count as one of them.

Old stories of ancestors
    From many years ago,
And of the family members
    Whom I had learned to know;

Who live no more among us
    And from our sight have gone,
But still the tender stories
    And memories live on.

Sometimes with dreamy musings
    I step into the past
And yield to the emotions
    These mem'ries o'er me cast.

Laughing at funny stories,
    Learning from their mistakes,
Yielding to pulses of courage
    The tale of their triumph awakes;

Shedding a tear in silence
    When stories of grief are told,
Quoting many a proverb
    Remembered from days of old;

And when the present calls me,
    I put away my gem.
Old stories and sweet mem'ries,
    How I do treasure them!

From a Grateful Lover

by Vernon Miller

My Dear Alta,

An angel watched me day by day
To keep me on the narrow way -
Was it for nought that he did care?
That I met you, your friendship share?

Truely angels must have guided you
And kept you thus so pure and true.
Did they in vain their vigilance keep,
Do I in vain these blessings reap?

'Twas not for nought nor yet in vain
That God has kept us from every stain.
Have faith: 'tis God our lives has wrought,
Us drew to him, and together brought.

Our father wrote this for our mother.
He printed it by hand. He also drew the roses.

34

A Wedding Poem

--Vernon E. Miller

Down the path of youthful lives,
Roses bloom beneath blue skies,
Dreams that beckon ever on
Scale new heights with each new dawn.

Wildest oceans they will cross,
Arid deserts know no loss.
Arctic cold or tropic heat
They will conquer and defeat.

May each duty in love be wrought,
Teach new beauty in deed or thought.
Never to repine in sin,
Always thinking, "It might have been."

Angry words, oh! let them never
In this union ever sever.
At the ending of each day
May strength of oneness be their stay.

Committed then, in heart and hand
To trust, to love, to understand,
Growing in the art of caring,
Nurtured by the gift of sharing.

Through the days of warming spring,
May the brooklet ever sing,
And life pour forth a dawning truth
In the garb of joyous youth.

Through the summer's heat be sowing
Seeds of hope and trust be growing,
For fast the years of life are flying,
Softly, softly the night calls crying.

Autumn's harvest now at hand.
They shall garner what they send.
As more swiftly days fly by
Light grows dim and night draws nigh.

Then the toil of life is over
Under winter's snow white cover.
As they came, so may they end,
Heaven blest days and homeward wend.

Our father wrote this for a friend's wedding in 1984.

Life Is Not Fair

Life is not fair. I have a sturdy dwelling.
  I am well-clothed and very amply fed,
While many people shiver through the winter
  And slowly starve for lack of daily bread.

Life is not fair. So many friends surround me
  With gentle smiles, kind words, and helping hands,
While others live in lonely isolation
  Without a friend who cares and understands.

Life is not fair. I have two loving parents
  Who taught me of the Lord, His will, His way,
While many others know not of His love and mercy
  And many die without Him ev'ry day.

Oh, God, I pray Thee, give a humble spirit,
  A thankful, grateful spirit unto me,
And may I learn to share my many blessings
  With heart of eager generosity.

                    --Mary Miller 2002

Chapter Two

WORDS OF INSPIRATION

The old mill and spillway below the dam

Matthew XXII

37. Jesus said unto him, Thou shalt love the Lord thy God with all thy heart, and with all thy soul, and with all thy mind.

38. This is the first and great commandment.

39. And the second is like unto it, Thou shalt love thy neighbour as thyself.

The Summary

To work, to help, to love, to give
A kind act for a blow,
To be a trusting child of God,
To do the best I know,
To be a sympathetic friend,
To wear a sunny smile--
What more or better could one wish
To make one's life worthwhile?

--Mary E. Miller

Two Kites

On a windy day when the sky was gray,
  Two kites set out to fly.
Away they went till their strings were spent
  And halted their tour of the sky.

"This is no fun," said the restless one--
  A spirited, willful thing.
He twisted and turned, for how he yearned
  To free himself from the string!

The other one cried, "Be glad you are tied!
  Don't worry and wiggle and chafe.
The pull of the string is the very thing
  That keeps your journey safe."

But just as he spoke the kite string broke.
  Away the rebel flew!
"Oh, look!" cried he, "I'm free! I'm free!
  Dear Brother, I pity you!"

But the fun of the sport was very short;
  He fell in a whirling descent.
A ragged limb reached out for him.
  He was splintered and tattered and bent.

The other flew high in the wind of the sky--
  A steady, contented thing.
"I'm safe," murmured he. "How glad I can be
  For the steadying pull of the string!"
               -Mary E. Miller

C almly beholding the face of the foe,

O nward, yes, onward determined to go.

U nder God's hand it is useless to fear.

R ise, then, to conquer; the Father is near.

A ngels are camping on every side.

G od's is the battle, and God is the guide.

E ver take courage, and doubt will subside.

--Mary E. Miller

41

Scarcely sufficient to make it quite full.

Can't really say that the measure is whole.

All it would take is a little bit more,

Not really that much to settle the score.

This is the way of the miserly soul.

Having sufficient and plenty to spare,

Extra good measure, just, right, and fair.

Always poured out with great vigor and vim,

Pressed down and shaken and full to the brim.

If by such generous motives possessed,

Never begrudging to give all the best,

God alone knows how such lives have been blest.

Mary E. Miller

Having no longing for glory or fame.

Using all talents to honor God's name.

Making another's desires one's own.

"I" has no rights and its wants are unknown.

Loving, though hated, reviled, or ignored.

It is sufficient to be as the Lord.

Thankful for ev'ry rebuke and correction.

Yielding to God who alone gives perfection.

--Mary E. Miller

Praying that God will grant patience to wait,

Always with calmness of mind.

Trying to speak, though the pressure is great,

In tones that are quiet and kind.

Earnestly running to finish the race,

Not with complaint, but with song.

Calmly believing the gift of God's grace

Enables the weak to be strong.

-MARY E. MILLER

44

Happiness

Happiness is but a state
    Of the life within the mind.
Outward circumstances are
    To the outward life confined.

    The complainer still complains
        In the midst of wealth and ease.
    Discontentment often thrives
        In the lap of luxuries.

        But the one who trusts in God
            Through each heartache and distress,
      Still can find in spite of pain
          Some real cause for thankfulness.

                  --Mary E. Miller

I Timothy VI

6. But godliness with contentment is great gain.

7. For we brought nothing into this world, and it is certain we can carry nothing out.

8. And having food and raiment let us be therewith content.

Contentment

Numberless, Lord, are the gifts from Thy hand.
The value of them is untold.
Then why should I poutingly beg for the few
Thy love has seen fit to withhold?
If Thou wilt but teach me to treasure Thy gifts
To their greatest and fullest extent,
Complainings shall cease, and the thoughts of my heart
Shall be gladly, serenely content.

-Mary E. Miller

At the Checkout

--Mary Elaine Miller

She was standing in line
    with her grocery cart
When she felt a whispering
    tug at her heart.
She paid for her goods
    with a hurried air,
Then turned to a customer
    standing there.
"That's a beautiful doll
    you are holding," she said.
"Don't open your wallet.
    I'll use mine instead."

The lady's response
    was a stare of surprise,
And a glint of defiance
    came into her eyes.
"I'm giving this doll
    to my daughter," said she.
"No stranger shall take
    that priv'lege from me!"

Then the first lady spoke
    with a lift of her hand,
"Please let me explain
    for you don't understand.
God told me to pay
    for the doll you have here,
Then give it to you.
    Have I made myself clear?"

The lady responded
    by starting to cry.
She spoke with some effort,
    "My husband and I
Believe there's no God.
    We heard our girl saying
Last night in her bedroom
    As if she were praying,
'Oh, God, are you real?
    (How I wish I would know!)
Please send me a doll
    Of the kind I like so.'

"We wanted to show her
    how false and untrue
Is the talk of a God
    and what He can do.
We want her to trust
    in our love and our care,
Not dabble in something
    as worthless as pray'r.
So here is the doll,
    And you say that God spoke
And told you to buy it?"
    Again her voice broke.

****

This story is based
    on a happening true.
I wish we would know
    all the ending, don't you?
But it blesses our hearts
    to feel reassured
No prayer of a seeker
    is ever unheard.

48

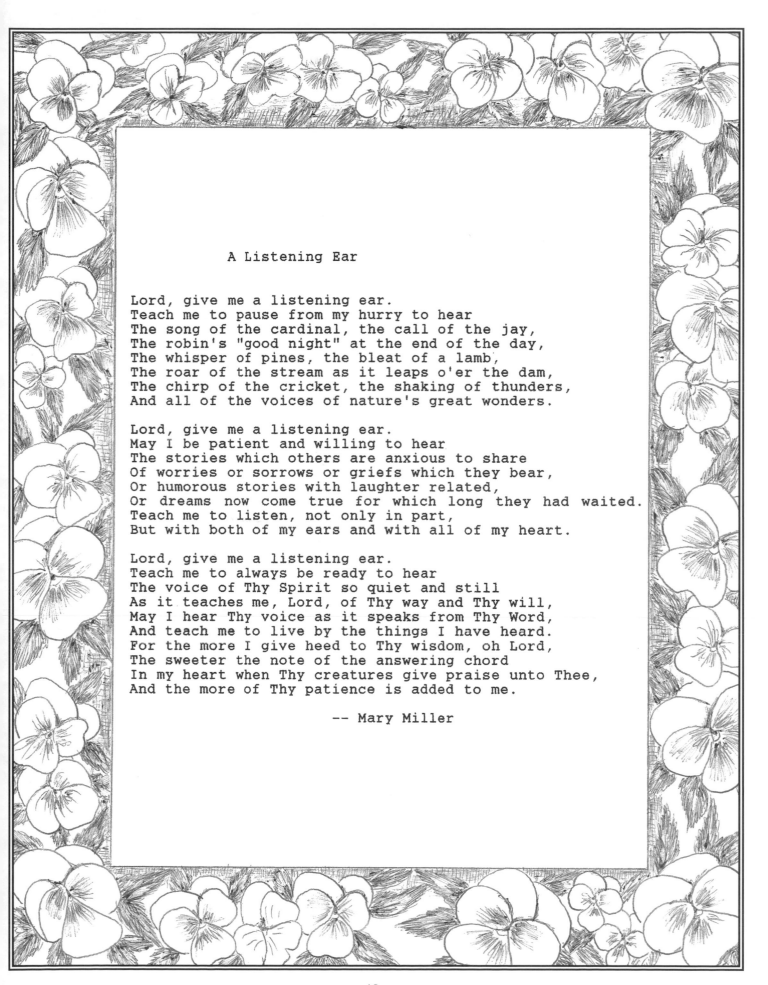

A Listening Ear

Lord, give me a listening ear.
Teach me to pause from my hurry to hear
The song of the cardinal, the call of the jay,
The robin's "good night" at the end of the day,
The whisper of pines, the bleat of a lamb,
The roar of the stream as it leaps o'er the dam,
The chirp of the cricket, the shaking of thunders,
And all of the voices of nature's great wonders.

Lord, give me a listening ear.
May I be patient and willing to hear
The stories which others are anxious to share
Of worries or sorrows or griefs which they bear,
Or humorous stories with laughter related,
Or dreams now come true for which long they had waited.
Teach me to listen, not only in part,
But with both of my ears and with all of my heart.

Lord, give me a listening ear.
Teach me to always be ready to hear
The voice of Thy Spirit so quiet and still
As it teaches me, Lord, of Thy way and Thy will,
May I hear Thy voice as it speaks from Thy Word,
And teach me to live by the things I have heard.
For the more I give heed to Thy wisdom, oh Lord,
The sweeter the note of the answering chord
In my heart when Thy creatures give praise unto Thee,
And the more of Thy patience is added to me.

                    -- Mary Miller

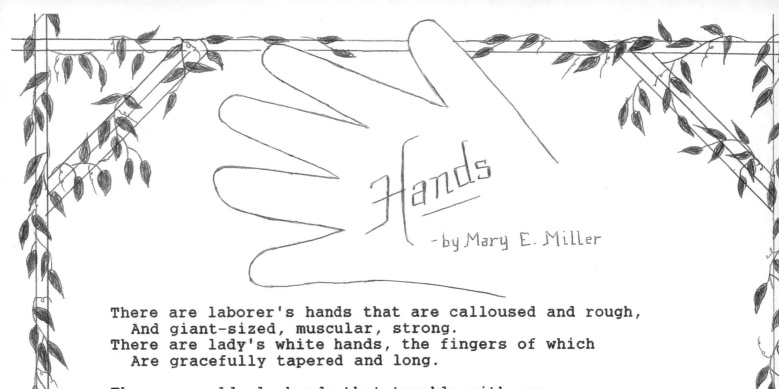

Hands

- by Mary E. Miller

There are laborer's hands that are calloused and rough,
  And giant-sized, muscular, strong.
There are lady's white hands, the fingers of which
  Are gracefully tapered and long.

There are elderly hands that tremble with age
  Whose fingers are bony and thin.
There are small baby hands so perfectly formed
  With delicate, rose-petal skin.

There are hands that have captured a beautiful thought
  And the thought on a canvas displayed.
There are hands that have wielded the needle and thread
  And many a garment have made.

There are hands of the genius which eagerly formed
  His invention, the child of the mind.
There are hands that have thoughtfully written great words
  To stir and inspire mankind.

There are hands that have faithfully guided the ship
  As she plowed her sure course through the main.
There are hands that have patiently guided the plow
  And hands that have cradled the grain.

There are hands that have rendered a sweet melody
  To which heart and ear have been tuned.
There are hands that have cooled a feverish brow
  Or skillfully sutured a wound.

There are hands that through which a strong courage has flowed
  To one who was trembling with fear.
There are comforting hands that have cheerfully sought
  To wipe from the eyes ev'ry tear.

There are hands that have held in a warm, friendly clasp
  The hand of the lonely and shy.
There are hands that have cradled the hand of the sick
  And of those who were waiting to die.

There are hands that are ugly and rough. There are hands
  Which posses little strength and no skill.
But the loveliest hands and the most useful hands
  Are the hands that accomplish God's will.

Humble Things

Some people have been blessed of God
　To speak great words sublime.
Their echoes wing their helpful way
　Through centuries of time.
The fame of some great noble deeds
　Has spread throughout the land,
And like great monuments of truth
　Inspiringly they stand.

But also it's the bits of good
　By but a handful seen,
The habits of a loving heart
　By Jesus Christ made clean;
The gentle words, the helping hand,
　The friendly smile, the nod.
Such things can, in their humble way,
　Reflect the love of God.

--Mary Elaine Miller

The solitary mountain peak
　Which stands against the sky
Lends inspiration to the soul
　And guidance to the eye.
But it's the tiny bits of soil
　Which yield the golden wheat
To give the hungry of the world
　Substantial bread to eat.

51

Recipe for

Bread

Mix together in large bowl:
2 tablespoons OR 2 packages active dry yeast
1 teaspoon sugar
1 cup warm water

Add
2 well-beaten eggs
2 cups scalded milk, cooled to lukewarm
3 to 4 teaspoons salt
2 to 3 tablespoons sugar

Stir in and beat until smooth:
2 cups whole wheat flour
1 cup white flour

Stir in and beat until blended:
2/3 cups melted shortening or vegetable oil

Work in
6 to 8 cups white flour

Knead for 15 minutes. Grease ball of dough lightly, cover, and allow to rise until doubled in bulk, 1 to 2 hours. Shape into loaves or buns. Allow to rise again. Bake at 375° until nicely browned. Remove from pans and grease tops of loaves. Makes about 4 one and one-fourth pound loaves.

Usually we make more than one recipe at a time--often four of them. That makes 10-12 loaves of bread plus cinnamon rolls, pizza crusts, dinner rolls, and/or hamburger buns. Our mother slices the bread before we put it into the freezer for later use.
                                                      Mary E. Miller

If Only the Best

If only the best of authors would write,
    How scarce the stories would be!
If only the fleetest of ships would sail,
    But few would travel the sea.

If only the best of musicians would sing,
    Most people would be without song.
If only the prettiest flowers would bloom,
    To whom would those flowers belong?

If only the very best player would play,
    What fun could he have all alone?
If only the liveliest brooklet would run,
    How many would hear its sweet tone?

If only the very best grain would grow,
    What flour could be used to make bread?
If only the best of the chefs would cook,
    What millions would be unfed!

So tackle the tasks which come to your hand
    With all of the talent you own,
And do not despair if you cannot excel,
    For the best cannot do it alone.

                    --Mary Elaine Miller

Cheerful Things

'Twas a little sunbeam
Shining through the pane
Made a dreary morning
Bright with hope again.

'Twas a bit of music
Of a happy song
Echoed cheer and gladness
All the morning long.

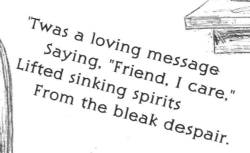

'Twas a loving message
Saying, "Friend, I care,"
Lifted sinking spirits
From the bleak despair.

'Twas a hearty handshake
With a friendly smile
Made that happy feeling
Linger on a while.

Let us sing that music.
Let us show we care.
Let us spread bright sunshine
On friends everywhere.

--Mary E. Miller

Chapter Three

THE GREAT
OUT OF DOORS

A Great Blue Heron

The Bird that Calls My Name

My name is Mary; do you know
Which bird it is that calls me so?
Why, it's the catbird, yes, 'tis he
That sings this special song to me--
    "Mary, Mary, Mary!"

I like to watch him as he flits
From twig to limb and how he sits
Upon a branch of some green tree
And says so unmistakably,
    "Mary, Mary, Mary!"

Sometimes he also says, "Meow!"
I always figured this how
The gentle catbird got his name.
His mate will answer him the same--
    "Meow! Meow!" then, "Mary."

Although most other birds display
More brilliant coats than his of gray,
I won't apologize for him;
He is so neat and smooth and trim
    And calls me, "Mary, Mary."

The cardinal with coat of red,
The chickadee with black-capped head,
The screaming scoundrel of a jay,
More kinds of birds than I can say
Are special in their own way, too.
But, Catbird, none can say like you,
    "Mary, Mary, Mary!"

I fancy I've a special claim
Upon the bird that calls my name.

    -Mary E. Miller

To the Robin

Silent Robin, on your nest
With your eggs beneath your breast,
Careful Robin, keep them warm.
Guard them well from theft or harm.
Do these brooding days become
Long and rather wearisome?
Bird, appreciate your rest
On your mud-daubed, stick-laid nest!
Soon your busy days will be
Brimming with activity.
Soon the little mouths will yawn
For a worm to feast upon.
And those mouths shall not express
One small word of thankfulness.
But those mouths shall all implore,
Gaping widely, "More! More! More!"
Without murmur you will drudge,
Not one worm to them begrudge.
But today upon the nest
Let yourself indulge in rest!

--Mary E. Miller

57

WELCOME, OH RED-WING!

Oh, red-winged blackbird, I am glad you're here!
    A cheering sign of spring you are to me!
I welcome your arrival every year.
Your happy warble floats so sweet and clear,
    "O-ka-leee!" Now listen, "O-ka-leee!"

You perch upon the cattail's slender stem
    And balance on the stalk so gracefully.
You like the marshes and you live in them.
There flashes on your wings a ruby gem.
    Oh happy red-winged blackbird! "O-ka-leee!"
                    --Mary E. Miller

THE FIREFLY

A gentle color lingers yet
Where in the west the sun has set,
And evening dusk begins to fall
And spread its shadows over all.
And now on every hand behold
The blinking lights of green and gold.

Oh, gentle little firefly
What memories of days gone by
Your shining light brings back to me!
How often I, with childish glee
And bare feet wet with chilly dew,
This little creature did pursue!
I'd single out one yellow light
And try to keep that spot in sight
While running. Then (unless I missed!)
I'd catch and hold him in my fist.
I'd watch him blink his light for me
Until at last I'd set him free.
I loved to watch him slowly crawl
Up to the highest point of all
Upon my hand, there to delay
A bit. Then he would fly away
To join the other fireflies
Or be another youngster's prize.

Oh, golden jewel of the night,
How glad I am to see your light!

--Mary Miller

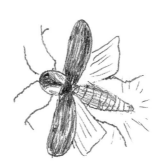

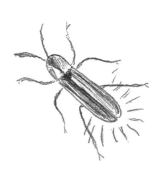

59

August 11, 1992--Tuesday: This morning was spent picking peaches in an orchard near Dowagaic, MI. The weather was pleasant for picking and for having a picnic at noon. We picked 42 bushels. Becky brought home a caterpillar (monarch) from the orchard. She calls him Tiger. He is a hearty eater.

August 17, 1992--Monday: Today Tiger turned into a chrysalis.

August 26, 1992--Wednesday: Becky's pet, Tiger is now a beautiful butterfly. She let him go this afternoon.

August 13, 2001--Monday: We picked 5 1/2 bushels of corn this morning, husked it, and cooked it. This afternoon while Mary was cutting off the corn, a friend called. She and her husband found 20 monarch caterpillars on their butterfly weed. They took them inside so they can watch them change into chrysalises, and then butterflies. She plans to give some caterpillars away and told Mary she thought it would be nice to include a poem. So while Mary finished cutting off the corn, she composed the poem. Ruthie delivered the poem this evening and was given a caterpillar.

How to Watch a Monarch Caterpillar Change into a Butterfly:
1. Look for a caterpillar with stripes of white, black, and yellow on milkweed or butterfly weed. (Drawings on facing page are of a monarch.)
2. Put it into a wide-mouth jar with holes in the lid for ventilation.
3. Put a small stick into the jar onto which the caterpillar can climb.
4. Feed the caterpillar daily with leaves from the same kind of plant on which you found it. It will have a big appetite!
5. When the caterpillar gets big enough, it will hang from the branch or jar. After a while it will shed its skin, and then you can see the chrysalis underneath.
6. Let the chrysalis hang undisturbed. It will stay that way about 10 days. On the day it is to come out, it will probably look black when you check it in the morning. If you look closely, you should see the black and orange on the wings. It usually emerges about mid-morning in 10 minutes' time.
7. You may take the butterfly out of the jar so it has room to exercise its wings. When your butterfly starts flying, take it outdoors and watch it fly away.

THE CATERPILLAR

The striped caterpillar
   Has such an appetite!
To satisfy his hunger
   He eats from morn till night.

And as he eats the milkweed
   Which makes him grow and grow
What would be his reaction
   If he would only know

What dreary fate awaits him--
   The chrysalistic tomb.
Would such news bring him sorrow
   And fill his life with gloom?

Or would he say, "Oh, listen,
   I wish, I long to be
A butterfly so graceful,
   So beautiful and free.

"The caterpillar then
   Will not exist, but I
Will wing and dip and soar,
   A happy butterfly!"?

The soul that longs for wings
   Above this world to rise
Cannot be free until
   His selfish nature dies.

When crucified to self
   He spreads his wings abroad.
He travels on triumphant
   Who gives his life to God.

                --Mary Miller

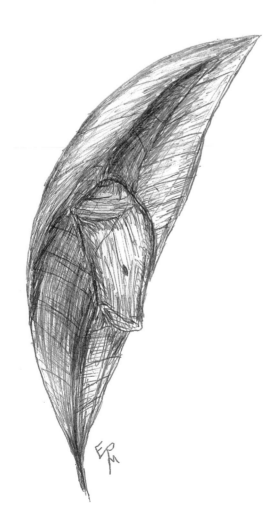

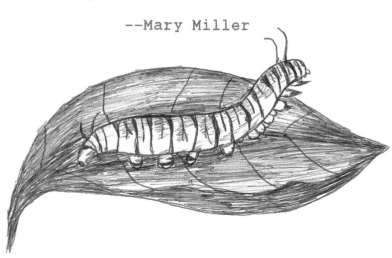

Excerpts from our Diary and Christmas Letters

May 31, 1999--Monday: On Saturday Mary discovered a hummingbird nest close to the chicken house with one navy bean-sized egg in it. Now there are two eggs in the nest.

August 27, 1999--Friday: A neighbor lady told us to count the chirps of a cricket in 15 seconds, add 37, and you will know what temperature it is. Ruthie tried it a couple times and it worked.

August 28, 2001--Tuesday: We have a trio around here that we have dubbed, "The Beggars." They are a mother mallard duck and her two ducklings. Sometimes they follow Papa and Sam to the barn in the morning, knowing they will be given some grain. Next they follow Sam to the pasture behind the house, hoping for another handout when he feeds the sheep. When the weather is so pleasant and the kitchen is cluttered from canning, we often eat on the patio. It seems "The Beggars" have this figured out because they are usually on hand, ready for the bread and corn we throw to them. They are so tame they will eat out of our hands, and when we sit on the ground, they crawl into our laps. If we hold a piece of bread above their heads, they jump up and grab it. The mother duck catches the corn we throw to her. Who could resist feeding such eager creatures as "The Beggars?"

September 7, 2001--Friday: This evening we saw a double rainbow for about 20 minutes. It was beautiful, the lower rainbow being especially brilliant. Once again we were reminded of God's promise.

May 17, 2002--Friday: On our way to the chores this morning we saw a pair of Canada geese with a gosling. The geese went ashore above the dam, but the gosling was swept over the dam. Below the dam the gosling went under the water a couple times. One of the parents swam out and broke the current so the little one could swim to the shore.

May 19, 2002--Sunday: Today we saw an indigo bunting on the bird feeder. We have been enjoying having hummingbirds, Baltimore orioles, red-headed woodpeckers, red-winged blackbirds, and rose-breasted grosbeaks feed in our backyard plus the regular callers like cardinals, chickadees, nuthatches and tufted titmice. Mallard ducks and fox squirrels eat the feed the birds spill. A young squirrel has gathered enough courage to come and eat.

Christmas letter, 1996,   There was excitement in the air as spring awakened the world after a long winter.   Anxiously we watched for the first robin, the tiny fuzz on the pussy willow, and the crocuses.   Later on we hunted for the mushrooms when the trilliums were blooming and the jack-in-the-pulpits were out. One mushroom measured about 8 inches tall.

We saw a scarlet tanager several times.   We were almost incredulous at Kathy's report of seeing a wild turkey and Mary's report of seeing a redstart.

Summer brought the wild raspberries for raspberry cream pies.   A mallard duck finally hatched out her young after her previous nests were robbed.   Perhaps a mink or a coon did the damage.   But there were plenty of ducks to paddle around on the mill stream.   One day we saw a blue heron watching the ducks fighting on the water.   It looked as if he would have liked to say, "Hey, what's going on here!"

A windstorm took down a big sycamore and a big elm tree the latter part of August.

Then fall came with all its color and beautiful weather. The goldenrod made the pasture look pretty.

To our surprise, a red fox appears to have its home around here.   The first time Sam saw him, he was carrying something (probably a rabbit) in his mouth.

The deer hunter has reported seeing a mother doe with four fawns on two different occasions.   He said they all tried to suckle the mother and seemed a little smaller than most other fawns for the time of the year.   Thankfully the hunter wants to shoot that deer family with only his camera and not his gun!

Once in awhile Sam will get out the telescope, and we look at the stars or the moon.   The detail we can see with the telescope is quite something.

The falling snowflakes, the frost-covered trees, and the hanging icicles all add to the splendor of the winter's wonderland and make the house seem warm and cozy.   We see tracks of many little creatures in the snow.

The bird feeder in our back yard becomes a very busy place. The fox squirrels are numerous here.   How they scatter when we come home from church!

When we see the marvels of nature, we surely can see there is a God Who is in control!   To Him belongs much glory and praise.

The Rosebush
by Mary E. Miller

Along a well-walked garden path
  A sturdy rosebush grew.
It nodded cheerfully to all
  Whenever breezes blew.
When it was calm, it stood erect.
  A pleasure to the eye.
It loved its work of spreading cheer
  To all the passers-by.
One day the Gardener came there,
  And with a trusty spade
He dug it from its well-loved place
  Where it had been displayed.
He took it to a quiet spot
  Where people seldom came.
The rosebush curled its petals up
  And drooped its leaves in shame.
"Have I done something wrong?" it asked.
  "What work can I do here?
I miss the people that would come
  To fill their hearts with cheer."
A little voice came on the breeze,
  "Friend, neither you nor I
Possess the right to question this
  Nor ask the reason why.
The Gardener does all things well.
  He is so wise and kind.
Uncurl your leaves, put down your roots,
  And you will shortly find,
If you but trust the Gardener
  Nor let your faith grow dim,
A steady purpose and a joy
  In blooming just for Him."
The rosebush took the words to heart
  And put away its grief.
It lifted up each blooming rose
  Uncurled each greening leaf.
It learned to love the Gardener
  In quite a deeper way,
And presently it found its joy
  Grew deeper day by day.
If it shall bloom for all again
  None but the Gardener knows,
But now it gives Him joy to find
  Submission in the rose.

A LESSON FROM THE FLOWERS

There are many kinds of flowers
  Which are lovely to behold.
Some are tiny; some are large.
  Colors range from pale to bold.

Lily-of-the-valley bells
  Delicate and sweet and pure,
Hiding in among their leaves
  Shyly bashful and demure.

Once the poppies start to pop
  They unfold without delay,
And their brilliant, showy cups
  Make a colorful display.

Flower made of many flowers
  Cluster in a lovely plume.
Lilacs load the soft, spring air
  With their gentle, sweet perfume.

Lovely is the queen of flowers,
  One that everybody knows.
Velvet-petaled, beautiful,
  Richly-scented is the rose.

Poor, unwanted dandelion
  Classified among the weeds.
Funny how its yellow top
  Soon becomes a ball of seeds.

There's the sunflower full of seeds
  'Round which grows a fringe of gold.
It will turn from east to west
  So it can the sun behold.

There are many, many more--
  Glads, petunias, hollyhocks,
Peonies, carnations, mums,
  Zinnias, marigolds, and phlox.

When our daily worries come
  There's one thought which sometimes springs
To the mind, "Does God the Lord
  Care about the little things?"

I would question all who would
  His most faithful care disclaim,
Why then did He not create
  All the flowers all the same?

          --Mary E. Miller with E. Ruth Miller

When we were small, we tried to press flowers. We carefully placed the flower between waxed papers and tucked it in a book. Then we stacked a pile of books on top and waited for it to dry. Usually we were disappointed because the flower turned out discolored and not nice. Eventually we found out that putting them between waxed papers held the moisture. The way we do it now is very simple.

Pressed flowers are nice for card making. (Look up "How to Make Greeting Cards with Pressed Flowers" in the index.)

Years ago, when photos were not so readily available, people would press flowers for a keepsake. Flowers with special sentimental value (such as one pressed from a funeral arrangement) were often kept in the family Bible.

How to Press Flowers:

1. Use a regular telephone book with newspaper-type pages. (Do not use glossy pages.) Gather flowers, preferably not during the heat of the day or while they are moist with dew or rain.
2. Lay the flowers out flat between the pages of the telephone book. Pansies work very well and so does Queen Anne's lace. Try different flowers and ferns. It is surprising how may kinds press nicely, but some will not.
3. Close the book carefully and let the flowers dry for at least 3 weeks.

How to Wax Leaves:

Caution: Do the following with adult supervision. Do not leave melting wax unattended. Do not melt wax in a pan directly over a flame, hot plate, or in a hot oven. If wax gets over heated, it can go into flames.

1. Find pretty colored leaves. Leaves from the sugar maple stay nice a long time.
2. Press them (see "How to Press Flowers" above) for at least 3 weeks, preferably a month.
3. Make a double-boiler arrangement with a skillet and an aluminum foil pie pan by filling the skillet partly full of water and placing the pie pan in the water. Melt enough paraffin or white candle wax to make 1/2 inch or more of liquid wax in the pie pan.
4. Spread newspapers on a table and carefully place hot skillet on a pot holder on the newspaper. Holding a leaf by its stem, dip the leaf into the wax. Remove and let excess wax drip into the pie pan. If possible, hang leaves with snap clothes pins for a few minutes for further drying. Occasionally you will need to place the skillet back on the stove to melt more wax or simply to keep it hot enough to spread evenly over the leaves. This gives the leaves a glossy finish and they stay nice for awhile. Waxed leaves can be stacked in a box if you are not ready to use them immediately.
5. Use a disposable paper background if you are using them for a bulletin board display. To affix leaves to board, simply apply a large drop of multi-purpose glue to paper and place leaf on the glue.

All in a Name

It grows in rolling pasture lands
    Where grass has not been mowed.
In weedy spots it shows itself
    It grows along the road.
Some folks regard it as a weed.
    And, yes, I would suppose
It wearies them to see how well
    The wild carrot grows.
But every summer when it blooms
    I hail it with delight.
I like the hundred tiny flowers
    So delicate and white.
They cluster in a round, flat disc,
    A sensitive, sweet face.
I know it's wild carrot, but
    I call it Queen Anne's Lace!

--Mary E. Miller

COLOR

The world would be a dreary sight
If colored only black and white
    With gray tones in between,
But God has made a lovely blue
To color the sky and the waters, too,
    And the summer grass is green.

Of yellow and red the flowers are made
And blue and purple of every shade--
    Some vivid and some duller.
The coat of the deer is a gentle brown.
The autumn tree wears a blazing gown.
    God's earth is full of color.

--Mary E. Miller

The Rainbow

On a wet and rainy evening
     In a wet and rainy spell,
When a pleasant week of sunshine
     Would have suited us full well,

I beheld a ray of sunlight
     Shining through the atmosphere,
And I wondered if a rainbow
     Might not presently appear.

Soon against the eastern background
     Full of clouds of gloom and gray,
There appeared an arching rainbow
     In a colorful display.

And I smiled as I beheld it
     With a sheepish sort of grin,
As I thought of what complainings
     I had been indulging in.

Rainstorms can be inconvenient
     When they drench a soggy land,
Or when work is interrupted
     By a rain we had not planned.

Still God sends His rainbow promise
     Made to Noah long ago.
This unpleasant, soggy weather
     Must find pause at last we know.

Shall the storms our lives must weather
     Cause our trembling faith to drown?
God has promised to uphold us.
     He will never let us down.

                    --Mary E. Miller

When More Rain Fell

For several weeks it had been dry.
The sun looked down from an arid sky.
We longed for rain with a wishful sigh.
   Rain fell at last.
We turned our minds from a desert scene.
The soil turned dark, and the grass turned green.
The dust was gone, and the world was clean.
   The drought was past.

The clouds broke up, and the sun broke through.
The clouds sailed off, and the sky was blue.
Our lives were filled with zest anew,
   And all was well.
Then a gray line rose in the dark northwest.
Exuberant spirits were depressed.
But we clung to our patience and still felt blest
   When more rain fell.

And then we entered the tropical zone.
The sun steamed hot whenever it shone.
Our hopes for good weather were often o'erthrown
   By a distant rumble.
The lightning flickered and flared and flashed.
The thunder crackled and cracked and crashed,
And rain on the earth was driven and dashed.
   We tried not to grumble.

For it is good to see once more
That it is God Who ruleth o'er
All things on earth, on sea and shore,
   And heaven above.
His rule is great and endlessly long.
His heart is wise, and He does no wrong,
For great as His might, so sovereign and strong,
   Is His wonderful love.

     ---Mary E. Miller

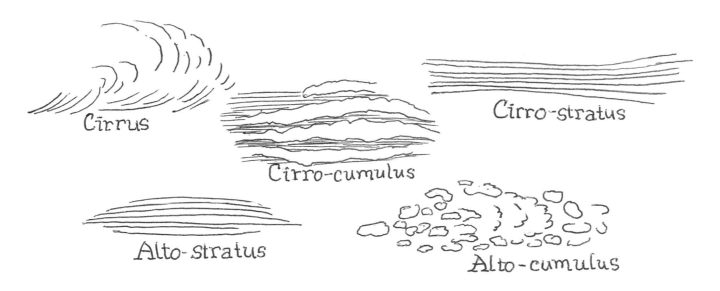

Cirrus

Cirro-cumulus

Cirro-stratus

Alto-stratus

Alto-cumulus

Casting shade upon the ground
Like a leafy tree.
Only they must wander on
Undetained and free.
Driven on by winds that fill
Sails of cloud-boats, never still.

Strato-cumulus

Nimbo-stratus

Cumulus

Cumulo-nimbus

Stratus

The Picture in the Millstream

A calm and quiet day,
      Well-lit with sunshine,
            Warm and cheery bright--

A sky whose puffy clouds
      Are few in number,
            Cottony and white--

A calm and quiet stream,
      A lazy millrace
            Flanked by banks of green

Where stand the trees,
      The golden maples,
            Stately and serene--

The water, like a glass,
      With clear reflections
            Hold the trees, the sky

And makes a double view
      Of all the color
            Which delights the eye.

            --Mary E. Miller

FROM SUNSET TO SUNRISE

The evening sun pressed
To his home in the west.
  The moon in the east rose higher.
The Queen of the Night
Was misty blue-white.
  The sun was a ball of fire.

The snowy land
Felt the sun's soft hand
  Touch it with gentle carressing,
As if the Day
Had chosen that way
  To render a parting blessing.

While the shadows that sift
From drift to drift
  Longer and bluer were growing,
The sunbeams which seek
To kiss the moon's cheek
  Had set its pale face to glowing.

And the sun sank low
Till even the glow
  That burns in the west had faded.
Then the moon, joining hands
With the starry bands,
  Through the streets of the heavens paraded.

And thus they marched on
Till the blush of the dawn
  Gave hint that the stars should retire,
Then the moon went to rest
In the hills of the west
  And the sun in the east rose higher.

                  --Mary E. Miller

The Sunset

In awe I watched the splendor
     of the winter's setting sun.
The lovely golden colors told me
     that the day is done.

The sky is red and orange
     and a shade of violet blue,
And yellow, green, and purple,
     and a lovely golden hue.

The trees are silhouetted
     against the colored sky.
The wind blows softly through their tops
     and hums a lullaby.

The snow reflects the colors
     of this truly awesome sight.
And then the colors start to fade
     with the coming night.

---Mary Miller
About age 10

Chapter Four

THE MONTHS AND SEASONS

Snow-laden trees along the pasture lane

Genesis VIII

22. While the earth remaineth, seedtime and harvest, and cold and heat, and summer and winter, and day and night shall not cease.

Anticipating the New Year

Isn't it nice to think ahead
  On all this year may hold?
What unknown pleasures may await
  To give us joy untold!

But thoughts of new years sometimes are
  Beset with morbid fears;
Who knows what sorrows, too, may wait
  To bring us pain and tears?

So let us live that we may have
  A faith calm and serene.
God's children have no need to fear
  The unknown and unseen.

                    --Mary E. Miller

He shall cover thee with his feathers,
and under his wings shalt thou trust:
Psam 91:4a

Confidence for the Future

The sum of the love ever felt by mankind
    Since Adam was formed from the sod
Could never begin to compare with the love
    Contained in the heart of our God.
The wonderful power displayed on this earth
    By man in all time and each land
Is feeble and lacking and weak when compared
    With the might of God's powerful hand.
Oh, I should not worry or tremble with fear;
    Uncertain the future may be,
For the mightiest hand and the tenderest heart
    Will go through the new year with me.

--Mary E. Miller

J oining the old to the first of the new,

A dding a year to the sum.

N ever before were these things brought to view--

U nknown are events yet to come.

A lways unchanging the day-by-day care

R endered with love to God's own ev'rywhere.

Y ears come and go, but God always is there.

--Mary E. Miller

Whispers of Spring

Something in the sky today
    Whispered, "Spring!" to me.
What it was I could not say
    With much certainty.
Was the sky, now mostly clear,
    Made of softer blue?
Did the lazy clouds appear
    Almost softer, too?
No, I could not say for sure
    What it was, but I
Thought I heard spring's messenger
    Whisper from the sky.

Something in the chattering
    Of the birds today
Really made me think of spring;
    Why, I could not say.
I had heard them chirp before
    All the winter long.
Was there maybe something more
    Hidden in their song?
Did a brighter energy
    Make a gladder tune?
Something in it said to me,
    "Spring is coming soon."

Something in the wind today,
    Soft, and almost warm,
Blew the winter's gloom away
    With a gentle charm.
Oh, how very good it felt
    As it touched my cheeks!
Told of snows that soon would melt,
    Told of rising creeks.
Something in it spoke to me
    Of the coming spring,
And I listened longingly
    To its whispering.

On the morrow clouds may rise
    Laden with more snow.
Winter's gloom may fill the skies;
    Bitter winds may blow.
Busy birds may search for food.
    Few the notes they sing.
Will the weather's changing mood
    Quench all thoughts of spring?
Though its coming may delay,
    Hope shall not depart.
For the spring has come to stay
    In each trusting heart.
                    --Mary E. Miller

March

by Mary Miller

March, March,
Triumphal arch
    Through which spring comes parading.
The cold and snow
Must shortly go
    For winter's strength is fading.

When robins sing
It feels like spring.
    They chirp and cheep and chatter.
The cloud-filled sky
Is seldom dry.
    The raindrops pitter patter.

The rain makes mud.
The rivers flood.
    The lakes and ponds are brimming.
Among the trees
The mallard sees
    Delightful spots for swimming.

The waning snow
Makes bare spots grow.
    The ice, too, is receding.
Warm weather may
Have come to stay,
    But March can be misleading.

The tree buds swell.
And thus they tell
    Where leaves will soon be growing.
The branches sway
And bend and play
    With March winds that are blowing.

The peepers wake,
And how they make
    A clamor with their voices!
The swamp abounds
With piping sounds,
    And all the marsh rejoices.

In flower beds
Courageous heads
    Of hyacinths are peeking.
The crocus cup
That opened up
    Of dauntless heart is speaking.

For many years
These harbingers
    Their message have repeated,
But ev'ry spring
Each old, new thing
    With joyful warmth is greeted.

Psalm LXV

9. Thou visitest the earth, and waterest it: thou greatly enrichest it with the river of God, which is full of water: thou preparest them corn, when thou hast so provided for it.

10. Thou waterest the ridges thereof abundantly: thou settlest the furrows thereof: thou makest it soft with showers: thou blessest the springing thereof.

11. Thou crownest the year with thy goodness; and thy paths drop fatness.

12. They drop upon the pastures of the wilderness: and the little hills rejoice on every side.

13. The pastures are clothed with flocks; the valleys also are covered over with corn; they shout for joy, they also sing.

Spring

The robin hops across the lawn
  With such an air of happy cheer.
May we assume that winter's gone,
  And pleasant spring is really here?

The card'nal who, all winter long,
  Against the white displayed his red,
Has put away his winter song
  And sings his summer tunes instead.

At first the pussies shyly peered
  From willow branches, smooth and brown,
Now by spring weather warmed and cheered
  They flaunt their puffs of fuzzy down.

Well-hidden from exploring eyes
  The peepers group by marshy ground.
From thence their choruses arise—
  A genuinely springtime sound.

Where sunny rays have been soaked up
  In places sheltered from the cold,
There first is found the brave, bright cup
  Of crocuses of cheery gold.

And dreams and fancies, long asleep,
  Receive a fresh awakening.
And thoughts run free as winds that sweep
  Across the fields, for it is spring!

--Mary E. Miller

They Come!

--Mary E. Miller

From southern homes on joyful wing
Birds come to build their nests and sing.

From seeds that looked so brown and dead
Each spunky seedling lifts its head.

From muddy holes or warming lakes
Come turtles, frogs, and crawling snakes.

To longer days the cheerful sun
Returns, his winter journey done.

From snug, confining winter holes
Come hungry, furry animals.

The trees, once brown and bleak and bare,
Wave budding branches in the air.

From dormant bulbs and sleeping roots
Emerge the hardy, greening shoots.

From winter days now wearisome
We turn with joy for SPRING HAS COME!

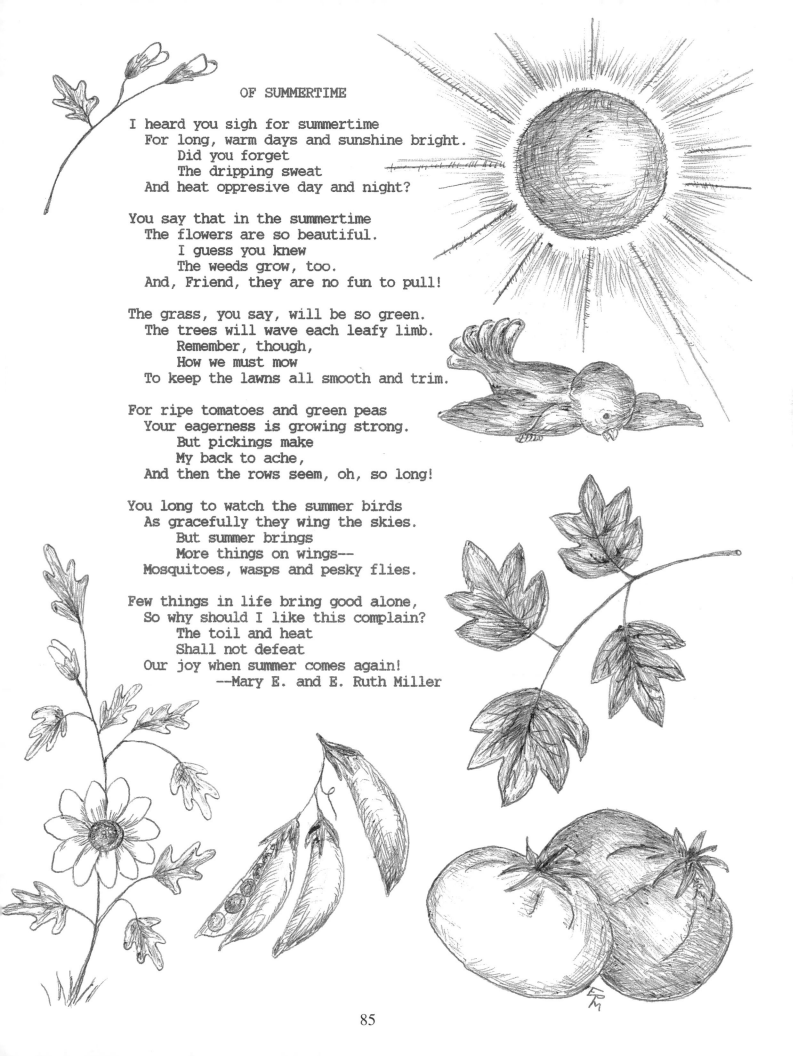

OF SUMMERTIME

I heard you sigh for summertime
    For long, warm days and sunshine bright.
        Did you forget
        The dripping sweat
    And heat oppresive day and night?

You say that in the summertime
    The flowers are so beautiful.
        I guess you knew
        The weeds grow, too.
    And, Friend, they are no fun to pull!

The grass, you say, will be so green.
    The trees will wave each leafy limb.
        Remember, though,
        How we must mow
    To keep the lawns all smooth and trim.

For ripe tomatoes and green peas
    Your eagerness is growing strong.
        But pickings make
        My back to ache,
    And then the rows seem, oh, so long!

You long to watch the summer birds
    As gracefully they wing the skies.
        But summer brings
        More things on wings--
    Mosquitoes, wasps and pesky flies.

Few things in life bring good alone,
    So why should I like this complain?
        The toil and heat
        Shall not defeat
    Our joy when summer comes again!
                --Mary E. and E. Ruth Miller

85

The Opening of the Evening Primrose

9:29 P.M.   9:31 P.M.   9:32 P.M.   9:32 P.M.   9:33 P.M.

JULY

When the sun arises early and the evening hours are long,
When cicadas start their buzzing and the crickets chirp their song,
When the lightning bugs are rising in the hot, oppressive nights,
And they show the blinking, blinking of their greenish-yellow lights,
When the trees are green and greener, though the grass sometimes is brown,
Till the thunderheads come rolling with a welcome cooling down,
When the trumpet vine is sounding in its silent, pretty way,
And the ground beneath is littered with the blooms from yesterday,
When the primrose thrills its watchers with its speedy open up,
Just a few breath-taking moments from tight bud to wide gold cup,
When the daily fare at dinner is delicious corn-on-cob,
When employment in the garden is a never-ending job,
When the fresh green beans are hanging, long and slim and right to pick,
When raspberry caps have blackened while the canes reach out to prick,
When the rye is bravely sprouting in the freshly-tilled pea patch,
When the cucumbers lie hidden underneath the leaves that scratch,
And the kitchen smells of onions, turmeric, and vinegar,
And the pickles in the fruit room wait consumption through the year,
When the bushes in the lowlands show their round blueberry fruits,
When potatoes can be stolen from among the spreading roots,
When the cattle seek the shade trees and lie down with blowing sighs,
As they graze, their tails are busy swishing, swishing pesky flies,
When the field corn reaches skyward, quickly growing past knee-high,
Then we know that it is summer; these things happen in July.

--Mary Elaine Miller

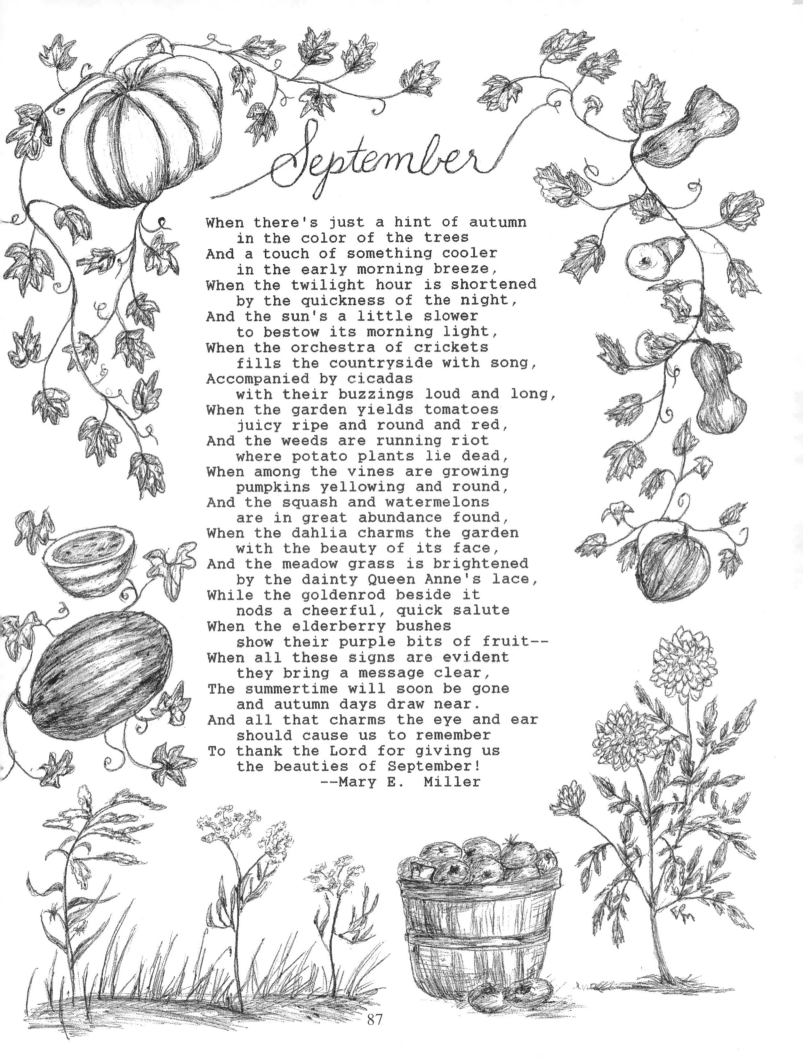

September

When there's just a hint of autumn
    in the color of the trees
And a touch of something cooler
    in the early morning breeze,
When the twilight hour is shortened
    by the quickness of the night,
And the sun's a little slower
    to bestow its morning light,
When the orchestra of crickets
    fills the countryside with song,
Accompanied by cicadas
    with their buzzings loud and long,
When the garden yields tomatoes
    juicy ripe and round and red,
And the weeds are running riot
    where potato plants lie dead,
When among the vines are growing
    pumpkins yellowing and round,
And the squash and watermelons
    are in great abundance found,
When the dahlia charms the garden
    with the beauty of its face,
And the meadow grass is brightened
    by the dainty Queen Anne's lace,
While the goldenrod beside it
    nods a cheerful, quick salute
When the elderberry bushes
    show their purple bits of fruit--
When all these signs are evident
    they bring a message clear,
The summertime will soon be gone
    and autumn days draw near.
And all that charms the eye and ear
    should cause us to remember
To thank the Lord for giving us
    the beauties of September!
                    --Mary E. Miller

October

October skies may be as deep a color
   As blue displayed by morning glory flowers,
Or blue-white in the hazy, warmer weather,
   Or smoky gray when bringing autumn showers.

October sunsets draw the blue-black shadows
   Across the land when daylight flickers low,
While in the west behind the thinning treetops
   The clear horizons shows a golden glow.

October foliage flaunts the flaming colors
   Of blazing bronze and gold and scarlet red,
While underneath the trees in bright confusion
   Are fallen leaves upon the grasses spread.

October mornings throw the blushing sunshine
   Against the purple clouds which line the west.
These circumstances give the autumn colors
   The light and background which display them best.

October weather may be warm and lazy
   With hazy sunshine in the afternoon,
Or brisk and chilly and invigorating
   Reminding all that winter's coming soon.

October is a month of brilliant beauty.
   When one enjoys the scenery day by day,
A time to feast the eyes on all the colors
   Before November blows the leaves away.
                --Mary E. Miller

If I'd Go Hunting

If I'd go hunting to hunt deer,
I'd watch for them where the water's near.
I'd quietly sit on the stump of a tree
Watching the creatures all about me.
The chipmunk would be eating close by
While a blue jay would scold somewhere high.
While I'd be watching so intently,
I'd lay the gun down ever so gently.
I'd hear a woodpecker pecking a tree--
Oh, there's so many things I'd hear and see!
When out of the woods comes a lovely deer,
Down to the water with eyes full of fear.
I'd hold my breath, not making a sound,
While the doe would carefully look around.
She'd take a long drink--long as she'd dare
Then she'd be off with tail in the air.
Dinner time then, for high is the sun.
I'd hurry right home, then remember my gun!

--E. Ruth Miller

Languid or lively, depending on the wind,

Eddying downward, downward to the ground.

After all summer to the branches pinned

Venture they forth in freedom newly-found.

Each with a glory no work of man achieves.

Summer has ended; autumn stole the leaves.

– MARY E. MILLER

Blooming in November

Bravely uplifting each bright, frilly head,
Changing from yellow to orangish-red,
While other flowers are dying or dead,
    This is the mum in November.

Beautiful roses, delighting the eye,
Cheering the spirits of all who pass by,
Blooming undaunted though winter draws nigh,
    Bloom, Rose, bloom on in November.

Tiny white flowers as white as the snow,
Thousands of flowers in borders that grow
Splendidly wide, but creeping and low--
    Alyssum still blooms in November.

Late in life's autumn some pleasures have flown,
Yet the best pleasure that mortals have known,
Walking with God who takes care of His own,
    Still may bloom on in November.

Cultivate well and protect from all harm
Loving impulses, kind, generous, warm,
That with great beauty and delicate charm
    Joy may bloom on in November.

Bloom on, oh virtues of truth and of peace!
Beautiful virtues that never will cease
But will in heaven their beauty increase
    After, long after, November.

        --Mary Miller

The Contrast

It was a late November day.
  A heaviness appalling
Was thickly felt. A dreary rain
  Had shortly ceased its falling,
As if the clouds, still thickly hung,
  Of strength had been depleted,
And, brooding o'er their troubles, felt
  Discouraged and defeated.
The air was sickly warm and damp.
  The autumn wind had taken
The heavy foliage from the trees
  And left them bare, forsaken.
In scattered heaps upon the ground
  The soggy leaves were lying,
With all the air of those who know
  There's nothing left but dying.

A couple days have passed. The sun
  Upon the earth is shining.
What happy changes have been wrought
  Where all was once repining!
The gloom and dread the cheerful rays
  Are busily erasing.
The blue, blue sky is free of clouds.
  The air is crisp and bracing.
The trees are lifting to the sky
  Their silver branches steady,
Declaring to all passersby
  For winter they are ready.
It seems within each wooden heart
  A patient hope is burning,
The confidence that in its time
  The spring will be returning.
Compared with several weeks ago
  The leaves are faded, duller,
But where the sunlight touches them
  They glow with gentle color.
Although the thought of certain death
  Still seems unkind and cruel,
Sweet hope has whispered to them, too,
  A promise of renewal.
Next summer's leaves will be more green,
  The violets bloom more sweetly.
For other plants shall feed upon
  The leaves decayed completely.

Illumined by God's holy light,
  Convinced of His sweet caring,
Shall there be room for gloomy dread
  Or hopeless, bleak despairing?
When disappointments come, may hope
  Still be anticipating
The sweet fulfillment of those dreams
  Made better by the waiting!
And if a dream should never come
  To happy realization,
Let not sad bitterness arise
  From thwarted expectation.
Our God can do such wondrous things!
  From buried dreams arising
May come sweet blessings manifold
  In manners most surprising.
Oh, may such miracles awake
  Our souls to each endeavor
To make the Lord our trust, our hope,
  Our aim, our life forever!
                    --Mary E. Miller

T ell me what you're thankful for--
H ome and clothing, house and friends,
A ll the fruits of garden's store
N ow brought in when summer ends,
K in with which to share this day,
S uch a feast before us spread!
G od has blessed in ev'ry way
I t is by His hand we're fed.
V erily God's gift, His son,
I s what makes our life worth living.
N ow let's praise Him, ev'ryone,
G ratefully with true thanksgiving.

--Mary E. Miller

Excerpt from our Christmas Letter

Christmas letter, 2001:   Thanksgiving Day is a favorite time of the year for our family.   Food preparation begins the day before so the big Thanksgiving meal arrives on the table in good order. By now we usually have our own specialties.   Kathy puts the cranberries through the grinder and grates the apples for the cranberry salad.   Becky peels the Irish potatoes and the 3 kinds of sweet potatoes she raises in the garden.   Mama and Mary bake the apple, mince, and pumpkin pies.   Ruthie stirs up the dressing and stuffs the turkey. (Last year she had to stuff it twice because she forgot one of the ingredients the first time.) The turkey goes into the oven at 5:00 in the morning.

We put two tables together to make one large table and set it with Great Grandma Holdeman's dishes. Besides the afore-mentioned foods; gravy, dinner rolls, lettuce salad, last of the garden, and homemade ice cream are added to the bounty.   Our guests are friends and cousins. Last year there were 18 of us seated around the table. Before the blessing, we sing a Thanksgiving song of praise.   Then we enjoy the food, and the pleasant conversation continues late into the afternoon.   There are many blessings to be thankful for on this day and the whole year through.

Thanksgiving Blessings

--Mary Elaine Miller

There's a warm and cozy feeling
    That delights us ev'ry year,
When October has departed
    And Thanksgiving time draws near.

When the low, gray skies are dark'ning,
    And the wind blows damp and chill,
Roaring down the old brick chimney,
    Whistling at the window sill,

Then how pleasant to be seated
    By the woodstove's crackling heat,
Till that damp, cold feeling leaves you,
    And you're warmed from head to feet.

What a pleasure to remember
    All those hours of sweaty toil,
Planting, hoeing, picking, pulling,
    Reaping produce from the soil.

In the cellar are the fruit shelves
    Lined with food in many jars.
We are thankful when we think of
    All the blessings that are ours!

Stuffed Turkey

Mama says we should be thankful
    Every day throughout the year
Not just wait until Thanksgiving.
    And although she's right, I'm sure
I am glad we have Thanksgiving,
    And it isn't far away.
For, you see, I like the dinner
    Mama serves Thanksgiving Day.
Sis and Mama have been busy
    Getting ready for our feast.
I'm their right-hand man and helper,
    Mama says I am at least.
I'm not sure Sis always thinks so--
    If I spill, she's apt to scold,
Calls me, "Careless Little Billy."
    Little! Why, I'm five years old!
I can stir and beat and measure,
    I can sample, too, and taste.
I can lick the empty dishes
    So no scrapings go to waste.
And I like to watch my mama
    Turning pumpkins into pie.
When she's busy peeling apples
    I sneak pieces on the sly!
"Now I'm going to stuff the turkey.
    Want to watch me?" Mama said.
So I watched in round-eyed wonder
    While she mixed the eggs and bread
And the celery, sage and onions.
    This she spooned into the hole
That's inside that great big turkey
    Till he was completely full.
Then she sewed him shut (How funny!)
    With a needle and a thread.
Made me think of how my granny
    Stuffed the pillows for my bed.

Then at last it was Thanksgiving.
    After greeting every guest,
Uncle Peter and his family,
    Granny, Mabel, and the rest,
We all headed to the table,
    Everybody found his place.
While we bowed our heads in silence
    Uncle Peter said the grace.
Then we passed the steaming dishes.
    Food was heaped on every plate.
Then I wish you could have seen us!
    How we ate, and ate, and ate!
Mashed potatoes, sweet potatoes,
    Turkey with its stuffing--yum!
Gravy, rolls, cranberry salad--
    Of each dish I wanted some.
Golden pumpkin, spicy mincemeat,
    Juicy apple pies were passed.
Which to choose? They looked delicious--
    Each more tempting than the last.
So I took three nice-sized pieces.
    Soon my tummy felt so tight.
Leaving food is very wasteful.
    Mama says it isn't right.
So I slowly, bravely ate them.
    Bite by bite I put them in.
Till I felt I was completely
    Filled with food from toes to chin!

Mama said she'd stuff a turkey.
    Well, she did. It's also true
That by serving such a dinner
    My dear mama stuffed me, too!
--Mary E. Miller and E. Ruth Miller

An imaginary story

96

SNOWFLAKES

Snowflakes are tiny
   And delicate things.
They float from the heavens
   On icy cold wings.

How pleasant the journey
   From sky to the ground!
They ride on the breezes
   And flutter around.

Each one has a six-sided
   Dazzling white face,
More daintily patterned
   Than intricate lace.

They tuck all the landscape
   In covers of white,
And quietly rest
   Through the long winter night.

Awake, every snowflake!
   The bright morning sun
Has sent invitations
   To join in the fun.

Each flake is as bright
   As a diamond or gem
When sunbeams are playing
   And dancing on them.

At last when the snowflakes
   Are tired and gray
The sun and warm breezes
   Dissolve them away.

Oh, are we not thankful
   To God that He makes
Such wintertime treasures
   As tiny snowflakes!

                --Mary Miller

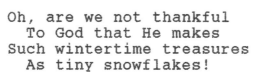

Excerpts from our Diary and Christmas Letters

December 25, 1996--Wednesday: Christmas Day. We opened our gifts at breakfast. For dinner we invited our neighbor, Larry, and Great Aunt Ella. Michelle, Bryan, Andy, and Timmy, children we babysit, were here for a candlelight supper. We enjoyed different foods given by friends--ham smoked over corn cobs, a cheese ball, popcorn, peanuts, cookies, and candy. We also had Becky's fruitcake and pizzelles, a fancy Italian cookie, that Ruthie and Kathy made yesterday. We had a white Christmas.

December 17, 1999--Friday: We have been baking some cookies this week to give away for Christmas. We made peanut butter, raisin-filled, and thumbprint cookies earlier, and today we finished with chocolate chip and velvet cookies. We also made a batch of fudge.

December 25, 2001--Monday: Christmas day. We had a pleasant day at home which started out with the rare treat of sleeping in. We enjoyed eating some of the goodies our friends have been giving us. We had 10 guests for dinner.

December 25, 2002--Wednesday: Christmas Day. Around 8" of snow fell during the night so everything was so white and beautiful. We had a pleasant day with plenty of good food. After breakfast we opened our gifts. We read, rested, wrote letters, made cards, and sang. In the afternoon Ruthie sculptured a polar bear in the snowbank. She also made the heads of a dog, cat, pig, and rabbit.

****

January 1, 1999--Friday: New Year's Day. We have invited Uncle Don, Aunt Madge, and their family for dinner tomorrow and are expecting 19 guests. The turkey is stuffed, the Irish and sweet potatoes are peeled, the salad is made, and the cookies and raspberry cream pies are baked. In the evening Papa has been reading to us from the book, *Echoes of the Past*, a collection of short stories from years ago written mostly by Amish people. Tonight the article he read told about a snowstorm they had when the author lived in North Dakota. A farmer was coming home in an open bobsled when the horses stopped. Believing they were worn out, he turned the bobsled over and crawled in for the night. In the morning he discovered they were right in front of their own barn doors! We wondered what the horses thought.

January 2, 1999--Saturday: It snowed during the night and it continued all day! It was decided to postpone our meal until next Saturday. Mama carved and froze the turkey for next week, and we are saving the cookies, but we plan to eat the rest of the food. We shouldn't have to cook much for awhile! Sam measured about a foot of snow tonight, and it is still snowing!

The Christmas Spirit

The friendly Christmas spirit
 Has gone from door to door
In towns and in the country
 To bring us joy once more.

It makes the passing stranger
 Seem almost like a friend.
It multiplies the greetings,
 And smiles have no end.

It speaks of cheerful giving,
 And, "Peace, goodwill to men."
But when the season's over,
 Where is this feeling then?

Oh, that the Christ-like spirit
 Would have the strength and sway
The pleasant Christmas spirit
 Holds o'er our land today!

Then peace and love would render
 Their blessings deep and true,
And melodies of gladness
 Would last the whole year through!

--Mary Elaine Miller

Chosen of God to descend to this earth.

Heaven rejoiced when a virgin gave birth.

Rude was the stable, but angels applaud

Israel's seed and begotten of God!

Sought by the shepherds and worshiped with joy.

Truly a wonder, this sweet baby Boy.

Mary's heart pondered each stirring event.

All to God's glory that men could repent.

Savior, Redeemer, best Gift ever sent!

M.E.M.

Chapter Five

LIFE ON THE FARM

The barn

Milking the cow was Papa's job when I was a young girl. The summer I was 15, I was determined to learn how to milk. I became no expert at that time, but I could struggle through a milking when necessary. Later we had a cow that was a hard milker, and one of us would milk on the one side while Papa milked on the other. That was good practice for us. Our cow died in May of 2004, and, because of Papa's illness, we decided not to buy another one at that time. I often looked at the empty cow stall and wondered if we would ever have a cow again. How happy we were when Patience arrived in April of 2006! Having our own cow takes a lot of time and effort, but we certainly enjoy the milk and dairy products.

We keep several half-gallon jugs of ice in the freezer. After the milk is strained, we put two of them directly into the bucket of milk. This cools it quickly. We also use a couple to cool the cream after it has been heated.
Mary E. Miller

Recipe for
Butter

Heat cream to 161°. Hold temperature there one minute, and then cool quickly. Heating the cream keeps the butter fresh longer.

To churn, the cream should be 56° to 60°. Use the cooler temperature if the weather is hot. If you have no regular churn, you can make butter using the blender, electric mixer, or by shaking the cream in a jar.

After the butter has formed, pour off buttermilk. Put butter into bowl, adding cool, clean water and work it, using clean hands or the back of a spoon. Pour off water, add more clean water, repeat until water runs mostly clear. Add salt to taste. (Start with 1/2 teaspoon salt to one pound of butter.) If you have a wooden mold, soak in cold water (only for a minute or so) before filling with butter.

That Stubborn Cow

We had planned a picnic supper,
    And I thought it would be fun
When the men came home from Greencroft
    To announce, "The milking's done!"
If the milking would be finished
    We could linger o'er our food,
And we could enjoy the evening
    In a calm, unhurried mood.
Ruthie kindly said she'd help me.
    At five-thirty by the clock,
I was heading for the pasture
    Where we keep the dairy stock.
When I called the cow, she lifted
    Up her head and looked at me.
How I wished she'd heed my summons!
    But she stood there stubbornly.
Well, no use to stand and call her
    So I hurried to the spot
Where she stood and chased her northward
    Half the distance of the lot.
She was slow, but we made progress
    Through the gate, across the drive.
Did she think it was too early
    To be milked at half-past five?
Ruthie waited in the barnyard.
    When we got her halfway through,
Her slow steps became more balky
    And, despite all we could do
In the way of slappping, pleading,
    Coaxing her with grain, and such,

Her steps forward were reluctant.
    Well, at least we gained that much.
Finally, when not too distant
    From the barn she turned around--
How discouraging the feeling
    To be losing hard-won ground!
What a strain upon the patience!
    "We give up!" we said to her,
"Since you are so very stubborn,
    Just go back to where you were."
So we tried to chase her southward
    To the pasture, but alas,
She just stood there, and exhausted
    We sank down upon the grass.
Down the driveway came an auto
    (It was six o'clock by then),
And I was a bit embarrassed
    To be caught thus by the men.
But Sam smiled to hear my story,
    And he took the cow in hand,
Waved a stick and, "Hud-up! Bossie!"
    This she seemed to understand.
How she marched straight to the stable!
    Just as pretty as you please,
And she gave no further trouble.
    We soon had her milked with ease.
Yes, it made me feel quite helpless.
    Guess it's just a tale to prove
How sometimes when we can't do much
    We need help to make things move.

--Mary E. Miller

Excerpts from our Diary and Christmas Letters

October 20, 1992—Tuesday: Mary has been doing the chores in the evening when work runs late in the mill. She says she doesn't tie the cow when she milks her. When she is done milking, the cow backs out of her stall, raises the hook on the door with her nose, and walks out. Mary is getting more efficient with the milking, and tonight it took her only half an hour to do the chores. It was suggested that she got a hold of Cornelius (one of the other cattle) instead of the cow!

September 30, 1999—Thursday: After a long day in the cider mill Papa thought it was so quiet while milking. He put his head against the side of the cow, and the next thing he knew he was waking up!

September 10, 2003—Wednesday: After supper Mary took slop back to dump at the apple pulp pile. The sheep were so greedy that they mobbed her. She did not want to run and possibly excite the sheep buck (that we bought Monday) but decided it would be okay. The next thing she knew she was on the ground. She hopped up, grabbed the buck around the neck, held his nose up, and hollered for help. Ruthie and Kathy heard her call. Ruthie started to her rescue. Kathy hollered to Becky who was across the bridge to get the men. Finally Becky understood and then hollered to Sam. He jumped on the bike and went to Mary's rescue. Papa had just finished the milking and did not hear the commotion, but the cow did. She backed out of the stall and knocked Papa over. Thankfully neither Papa nor Mary was hurt and Papa even saved the milk!

April 8, 2006—Saturday: Today, at last, our cow arrived. She is a small, pretty cow, and we named her Patience. At milking time, Andy, who came for supper after work, helped Sam catch her. Together they could hardly hold her so they tied her to a tree. [To our relief, she soon adjusted to her new home.]

February 14, 2007—Wednesday: On this wintry morning our cow had a pretty, little fawn-colored heifer calf. We named her Beauty.

October 3, 2007—Wednesday: As Sam and Mary were milking the cow this evening, Sam said, "If the cow would kick the bucket in the right direction, someone [Clara] would be happy." A moment later the cow kicked, Mary was partly drenched, and Clara disappeared out the door.

Who Gets the Milk?

Mary E. Miller

Our fawn-colored calf we left with the cow.
This plan has worked well, fairly well, until now.
It's really too much for six people to drink
Five gallons of milk in one day, don't you think?
But recently Beauty (through hunger or greed)
Has drunk up more milk and has left us in need.
When we with reluctance have parted the two
Beauty says, "Baah!" and the cow bellows, "Mooo!"
When Patience, the mother, no longer could wait,
She flipped up the latch, and she opened the gate.
Sam saw she was out in the strawberry patch.
He chased her back in, and he looked at that latch.
He went for a wire, and he came back right quick,
But she had already repeated the trick!
So now we regard her with greater respect.
Some cows cannot boast of such high intellect.
One Saturday morning was sticky and hot.
The calf bawled her grief from the south pasture lot.
At some little distance away to the north
The motherly answers came bellowing forth.
Perhaps if poor Beauty were next to the cow,
The pair would be quiet? We'd try, anyhow.
The calf did not know that we meant to be kind.
It took quite some effort to make her to mind.
At last we were nearing the gate to the pen
Hard by the north cow lot--close, closer--and then
The calf saw the object of all her desire.
She put her head down and ran under the wire.
I helplessly laughed and watched with a grin.
What now? Would the calf or the poor people win?
So then, though it was but the middle of day,
We milked. So we won by that much, anyway.
What moments were lost and what plans were upset
By such interruptions we tend to forget.
We have to admit, though, it's times such as these
That many years later make great memories.

Recipe for
Ice Cream

No need to crank an ice cream freezer with this recipe. Freeze in the deep freeze or in the freezer part of the refrigerator.

4 cups milk
1 1/2 cup sugar
1 tablespoon vanilla
3 rennet tablets (box says "for rennet custard and ice cream")
3 tablespoons cold water
4 cups whipping cream
1 3.4-oz. package instant pudding mix, any flavor (optional)

The pudding mix not only adds more flavor, but it also makes the ice cream a nicer consistency.

Heat milk until lukewarm, add sugar and vanilla, and stir until sugar is dissolved. Crush rennet tablets and mix with cold water. Stir into milk mixture and pour immediately into flat pan. Let stand undisturbed 10 minutes. Freeze.

Remove frozen milk from freezer. Let it soften a bit; then cut the frozen milk into chunks and put into a large bowl. Sprinkle the pudding mix on top. Whip the cream until stiff. Set aside.

Beat frozen milk on low speed with electric mixer. Stir in the whipped cream and beat until blended. Delicious served immediately. If you freeze it for later use, allow to soften at room temperature for about 30 minutes before serving.

(You will soon learn to adjust thawing time for frozen milk, depending on outside temperature. When it is really hot, set whipped cream into freezer while beating the frozen milk.)

Mama has faithfully made ice cream for us. When we were younger, we had ice cream for both dinner and supper. It goes really well with fruit, pies, and almost any kind of dessert.

Recipe for
Small Curd Cottage Cheese

Pour 2 gallons skim milk into crock or non-metal container. Stir in about 3 cups cultured buttermilk. Cover and allow to set undisturbed 36 to 48 hours until firm. Dip sour milk into kettle (save 3 cups for starter for next batch and keep in refrigerator or freezer) and heat to about 105°. Dip into cheesecloth-lined colander and allow to drain for several hours. Put curds into a bowl and crumble; stir in 1 teaspoon salt and enough milk or cream (perhaps one cup) to make desired consistency.

Recipe for
Slicing Cheese

Start making cheese according to above recipe, but heat curds to 170°. Drain. Add 2 1/2 teaspoons baking soda, and work thoroughly into curds. Allow to sit at room temperature for half a day or overnight.

In heavy Dutch oven melt 1/3 cup butter. Add curds and place over low heat, stirring frequently. When curds are melted (or nearly so) add 1/2 cup cheddar cheese powder and 1 teaspoon salt. Continue heating and stirring until smooth. Cream can be added if cheese is too stiff. Pour hot cheese into greased square pan. Refrigerate.

This cheese is good in sandwiches and delicious in casseroles. Extra blocks of cheese can be frozen for later use.

Years ago we didn't know what to do with all our buttermilk. Then we discovered it can be used in this recipe instead of regular milk.

Recipe for
Squeaky Brick Cheese

Pour two gallons skim milk into kettle. Heat to 90°. Stir in 1/2 cup cultured buttermilk or cottage cheese starter (see recipe for cottage cheese) and let set 30 minutes.

Add 1/2 tablet cheese rennet or 2 tablets rennet for rennet custard and cream. Tablet(s) should be crushed into a powder and mixed with a little cold water before adding to milk. Stir milk after adding rennet.

Let set 1 hour or until milk is firm.

Cut curds with long knife to make 1/2 inch squares. Now slant your knife to the right and cut along the lines that go back and forth. It is not necessary to cut those that go from side to side. Now slant the knife to the left and cut along the same lines again. The idea is to have the curds cut into small pieces. Let set 10 minutes.

Heat slowly to 108°, stirring frequently. The ideal rate is 2° every 5 minutes.

Drain through cheese cloth until it quits dripping. Put curds into bowl, crumble, and add 1 tablespoon salt and 1 teaspoon cheese herbs or spices of your own choice.

Put curds into cheesecloth-lined mold, apply pressure with hand. Let set 1 hour.

Gradually add weight until it totals about 4 pounds. You may use 2 quarts of water for the weight.

Air dry several hours, then refrigerate. Eat fresh.

BARN RAISING

No man by himself, though his muscles were strong,
Though he worked on it hard and he worked on it long,
Could have built a whole barn in the old-fashioned way
In which barns were erected in grandfather's day.
But by working together the great job was done,
No man giving more than the muscle of one.
What waits to be done for the cause of the right
Compared to the power of one person's might
Is so overwhelming it's tempting to say,
"Is there really much good one can do anyway?"
But no one is greater or lesser than you
For none can do more than one person can do.
Though few be the talents we seem to possess,
If we cannot do more, let's not choose to do less.
                    --Mary E. Miller

Little Lambs

Little lambs are charming,
    Loveable and cute,
Dressed in silken leggings
    And a woolen suit.

Long the ears and floppy,
    Smooth and black the nose,
From the eye what softness
    What a brightness glows!

Looking so contented
    Little lambs asleep,
Lying by their mothers,
    Big, fat, wooly sheep.

When the lambs are drinking,
    It's a funny sight,
How their long tails wiggle
    To express delight.

What a rare amusement
    Watching lambs at play!
Following their leader
    As he runs away.

Little hoofs go flying
    Down the beaten track;
Soon the lambs will circle
    And come running back.

It's so fun to watch them
    When they bounce around,
Holding all legs stiffly
    When they hit the ground.

How they seem to love it!
    As they run and jump,
Fighting for the kingship
    On a rock or stump.

When they are exhausted
    Down to rest they lie
While the mother watches
    With her wary eye.

Little lamb so playful
    In your woolen suit,
How could one describe you
    Otherwise than cute?

Mary Miller

Excerpts from our Diary and Christmas Letters

Christmas letter, 2004: When Bea was two days old, Mary brought her into the house, a very sick lamb. She sounded croupy so Becky brought out the vaporizer and set up a steam tent. The next day Mary brought Bea's twin, Vi, to the house also. Mary's good care of Bea and Vi paid off, and soon they were doing well. When they started crawling through the windows of their box, we decided it was time for them to spend the nights in the barn. They are still very tame, in fact, sometimes it would be better if they would be more timid.

Once when Sam put the sheep into the shed at night, Lorraine was missing. She must have been asleep among the willows.

April 24, 2004--Saturday: Around dark yesterday Bea and Vi met Kathy at the back door. They had somehow gotten through the fence. Today they got out again, and Bea started to nibble the tomato plants before Mary stopped her. (Becky had set the tomato plants outside the greenhouse.)

Christmas letter, 2005: Bea and Vi, our pet lambs from last year, are still pulling pranks. Bea was seen jumping over her sister, pretending to butt herself in a mirror, and pulling the string of the chainsaw with her mouth. One day after Vi had been nosing the tractor, Sam discovered the key was gone. To his relief, he found it on the ground.

February 19, 2006--Sunday: When Mary checked the sheep this evening, Marjorie was walking on her mother's back. Mary went outside to empty the water bucket. When she returned, Bea was just getting to a standing position, and Marjorie was jumping off! Bea is not the most dedicated mother, but the lambs are doing well. We think Marjorie takes after her mother.

March, 2008

03-03 Born to Marjorie: Forrest & Flora
03-03 Born to Bea: Elijah, Elisha & Eliza
03-04 Born to Lorraine: Evie
03-13 Born to Oreo: Minnie
03-16 Born to Vi: Joy and Jon

The morning after Minnie was born, Oreo, her mother, became excited when Sam went into the pen. She trampled Minnie and broke her leg. Sam brought Minnie into the house to be bandaged. Because of Oreo's record, we kept Minnie in the house. The break was in Minnie's upper leg which was hard to bandage. She was tiny and helpless and yet perky. She stood up by herself that day. Mama and Mary wrapped her leg every day, and on March 22, we saw her use it. A week later the splint fell off while she was running, and we did not replace it.

Our Pet Lambs—
BEA and VI

The lamb we brought into the house
    We thought would not survive.
But now we're happy to report
    She's very much alive.

Her croupiness has disappeared.
    Her cough has gone away.
You would not guess Bea has been ill
    To look at her today.

Her sister, Vi, was small and weak
    Though not as ill as Bea.
We brought her in, and now they keep
    Each other company.

Their clumsy mother stepped on Vi
    Behind her rib cage--ouch!
For days there was a swelling there.
    We called that lump a pouch.

But now that is much better, too.
    They're acting well and spry.
Although they are a lot of work,
    We're glad they did not die.

They have voracious appetites
    Which never seem to fail.
And when they eat, it's fun to watch
    Each wiggling, long black tail.

To always keep them in their box
    Would not be very wise,
And so sometimes we take them out
    To give them exercise.

They nibble on the furniture.
    They keep us on the run.
Sometimes we need to wipe the floor,
    But, oh, they're splendid fun!

They follow pretty well at times
    When we run down the hall.
Sometimes they heed, sometimes ignore
    Our voices when we call.

And when we put the lambs to bed
    They snuggle down to sleep.
Oh, there is lots of fun involved
    When one is raising sheep!

—MARY E. MILLER

RFD 2 BOX 580
LITTLETON, N.H. 03561
TELEPHONE 603-444-1050

Excerpts from our Diary and Christmas Letters

May 6, 2006--Saturday: Several years ago we looked into buying a llama to protect the sheep from dogs, but at that time they were too expensive. Today Sam and Mary went to an exotic animal auction where they bought a llama for $75.00. We named him Leo.

June 23, 2006--Friday: One evening Sam offered Leo some hay. Leo walked around the sheep, almost giving the impression that he was counting them before he would leave to eat the hay.

December 1, 2006--Friday: It was so cold that we tried to put Leo into the barn, but Leo had other ideas. We had him cornered by the stone pile, but he climbed over it. He did it very gracefully, too. Actually, with his fur coat he should be fine outside, and he can get some protection.

January 29, 2007--Monday: Leo appeared to have slept in the cattle shed with the cattle last night. We are glad he seems less afraid of the cattle.

February 20, 2007--Tuesday: After making cider today, we saw a squirrel helping itself to the apple pulp in the trailer. For the first time, Mary saw Leo eat apple pulp.

February 28, 2007--Wednesday: We turned the lambs out to pasture for the first time today. They did not want to leave the barn. Leo found them very interesting.

May 1, 2007--Tuesday: With Sam and Mary gone, we other girls are doing more chores than we usually do, and we find it both interesting and challenging. The beef cattle, the sheep, and the llama, 20 animals in all, are in the pasture south of the house. The sheep crowd in, greedily trying to devour the feed and hay. The cattle, who are fond of the hay, try to grab mouthfuls even before we feed them. Leo is much more polite. He likes the hay, but he will wait until we feed him.

August 19, 2007--Sunday: Since Sam and Becky were gone this evening, Kathy and Mary did the chores. When we went to feed the cattle behind the house, Heidi, Erin, and Beauty came out of the bushes and looked at us, but Fritz and Oscar were nowhere to be seen. Kathy went to find them while Mary waited. Once Mary looked behind her, and there was curious Leo only a yard or two away. When she sat down on the feed can to rest, four sheep came and wanted to be petted. They moved on and Linda, the sheep, wanted to be rubbed.

March, 2008: After dark one evening Sam had fed the cattle and was looking for Leo. As he was walking with Leo's hay, suddenly he realized Leo had come behind him and was nibbling the hay.

Leo

--by Mary E. Miller

Leo is a llama
    With brown, unruly hair.
He runs with easy motion
    And a smooth and graceful air.

We have a job for Leo.
    We bought him just to keep
The dogs and wild coyotes
    From preying on our sheep.

Among the flock he grazes
    And looks with watchful eye
For any harmful rovers
    Which may be prowling by.

The sheep no longer swelter
    At night inside the shed.
They sleep in cooler comfort
    Upon a grassy bed.

His ears stand straight to listen.
    His legs and neck are long.
Perhaps when we are absent
    He hums a llama song.

He has no hump to boast of
    So can it really be
That he claims to be a member
    Of the camel family?

At first he spooked the cattle.
    They ran away from him.
They seemed to think him something
    That threatened life and limb.

But now they roam the pasture
    And show no signs of fear
When Leo and his charges
    Come slowly grazing near.

We're glad we have our Leo
    To guard our little flock.
It also is exciting
    To have some llama stock!

Our Dog, Clara

--by Mary E. Miller

She's a very
good dog
and a funny one.
In summer she basks in the heat of the sun.
In winter she roasts by the blazing log,
And then we say, "Clara, you'll be a hot dog."
Of strangers' arrivals she thinks she must tell.
Sometimes she does it a little too well.
But, happily, most of the time she is quiet.
She has for a dog a very strange diet.
The plain, dry dog food she will not eat
Until it is slathered in some kind of treat,
Like leftovers, gravy, catsup, or such.
But dog food alone she simply won't touch.
She eats raw onions and peppers and peas.
Her eyes and her tail say, "More, if you please!"

Eating her food comes first (if it's yummy).
Next pleasure is getting a rub on her tummy.
It's funny to see her immobilized where
Sam let off his rubbing with legs in the air.
I give her a bath about once in a week,
And while I am scrubbing she's docile and meek.
But when we are done, you should see how she shakes,
And what a commotion and hubbub she makes!
She jumps in her box with a great, flying leap,
And paws at her blanket until it's a heap.
She runs to her dog dish and sniffs it for food,
And while in this frantic, indignant, wild mood
To ask for permission she boldly refuses
But jumps on the chairs or the beds as she chooses.
Sometimes to avoid all this ruckus I wrap
My dog in a towel and she sits on my lap.
We rock, and she groans in a sleepy delight.
It's kind of like purring in cats, but not quite.
She goes to her box when it comes time to pray.
She bows her head, too, sometimes, anyway!
When we work in the garden, she roams through the fields.
What a picture of happy dog life this scene yields!
Any small carcass she finds is a treasure.
She gnaws it and chaws it with great doggie pleasure.
I cannot explain the force which controls
My dog when in cow piles and such like she rolls.
I like her full well, and she dearly loves me,
But on this one point we cannot agree.
In spite of the risk of incurring her wrath,
I rinse her and scrub her and give her a bath.
She misses us sadly when we are away.
It seems that the loneliness felt through the day
Must plague her and haunt her far into that night,
For Mama oft wakes with her snuggled up tight
Against her in what was once Mama's clean bed.
Poor Clara is lonely, so what can be said?
Our cattle and chickens, our small flock of sheep
Must turn us a profit to pay for their keep.
Besides gladly cleaning spilled food off our floors,
Our Clara refuses to help with the chores.
She gives us no offspring or produce, and yet
She thinks it's enough to be only a pet.
We march to her drumming. She steps to our fife.
Who is it, pray tell me, that lives a dog's life?

Excerpts from our Diary and Christmas Letters

Christmas letter, 2004: Papa used to talk of having a little house dog and mentioned it again after he was sick. One Saturday some friends brought two little dogs into the house for him to see. When we saw how Papa enjoyed them, we decided to try to get a dog for him.

By Monday evening we had found a little six-year-old rat terrier, named Clara. We brought her home on trial, but it did not take us long to decide that she was the dog for us.

Papa liked Clara and she was good with him. We would put Clara on the bed with Papa, and she would lie beside him.

June 10, 2007--Sunday: Mary has been trying for months to teach Clara to shake hands before she gives her a treat. Since Kathy bought some better treats, the progress has seemed more rapid. Tonight Clara raised her paw before Mary was ready to give her the treat.

March, 2008: For weeks Mary has been trying to teach Clara to roll over. She did it for the first time on March 10. Everyone clapped and cheered. Later she grabbed her "fetch" paper and took it to Ruthie in the kitchen, dropped it, picked it up, and brought it back to Mary. Mary laughed and petted her, and she rolled over again! That called for another treat.

When we tell her to roll over, she acts like she is thinking hard, and then all at once she does it! Sometimes she will even do it without a treat.

July 31, 2006--Monday: When we pulled the peas earlier this month, we dumped the plants in the pasture south of the house. The animals formed a circle around the pile. 7 cattle were on one side and 13 sheep on the other. Leo, the llama, was nearby. The animals are so eager for any treats (our corncobs, etc.) that they can become a nuisance. However, Becky says that sometimes when she is pushing the wheelbarrow, Bea, the sheep, walks on her right side and Vi, Bea's twin, walks on her left and help push it.

September 7, 2007--Friday: Uncle Glenn and Aunt Norma Jean gave us a surprise visit today. Uncle Glenn, who is Mama's brother, has many interesting stories to tell. Today he told us how Great Grandpa John Henry Marks used to direct the men at a barn raising. A row of men would lift a beam to their shoulders with Grandpa John riding it. The next row of men would use short poles and raise the beam higher. By this time the first row of men had taken long poles to raise the beam on up. Still riding the beam, Grandpa John could shout down directions to get it into place. Grandpa John was probably only 5' 4" tall and weighed about 110 pounds so he was a good man for the job.

Pooch and the Cow

Once I watched a little dog
  That was fastened to a chain.
He leaned into his collar
  And he pulled with might and main.

He was barking at our cow.
  How he longed to give her chase!
But the sturdy chain and collar
  Held him firmly in his place.

And I wondered why this dog
  Could not see it would be best
To recline upon the greensward
  And indulge himself in rest.

In the pleasant air and sunshine
  He could revel at his ease.
There would be, for entertainment,
  Little bugs to sniff and tease.

Then I thought how very often
  I myself had done the same--
Pined for that which was denied me--
  And my head was bent in shame.

Thank you, Pooch, for this good lesson.
  May your fruitless struggles teach
Such as I to be contented
  With the good within my reach.

--Mary E. Miller

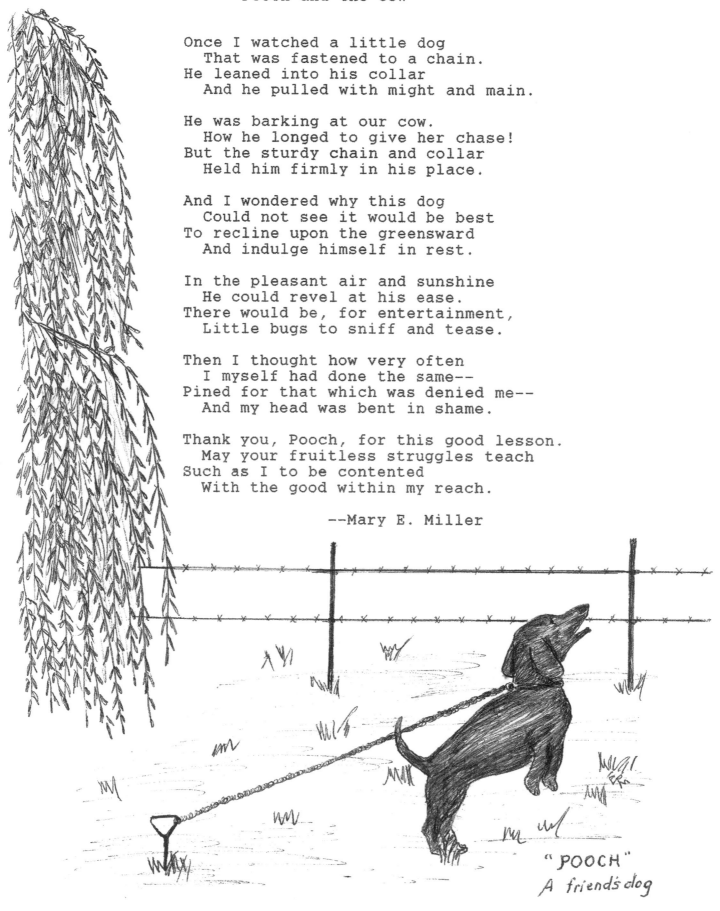

"POOCH"
A friend's dog

Excerpts from our Diary and Christmas Letters

May 14, 1996--Tuesday: 57 little chicks came to live in our brooder house today.   They are fun to watch--some of them go scooting around while others huddle together.

October 31, 1998--Saturday: Our 30 chickens laid 30 eggs today!

March 9, 2005--Wednesday: Mary brought the car over for Kathy after chores. She had one dog, 2 cans of grain, 3 empty water jugs, and 6 eggs (no egg basket) to transport. Clara, the dog, crawled into her lap almost right away. The eggs were rolling so at the bridge she held one in each hand. They arrived safely, no cracked eggs, and no spilled grain--until she lifted the can out of the car, and then she spilled just a bit.

May 4, 2005--Wednesday: Our thermometer showed 23 degrees this morning. When Mary checked the chicks (which we picked up yesterday), they were huddled together under the light. She brought them into the house and kept them warm by the stove.

Christmas Letter, 2006: One of the chickens was badly pecked so Mary put it into the old pig hut near the pile of apple pulp. One day she dumped the pulp, checked the chicken, found an egg, and put it on the tractor seat. Next she swept out the trailer. As she was driving toward the house, she thought, "What happened to that egg?" Sure enough, she was sitting on it.

February 8, 2007--Thursday: The rooster has been attacking the chicken house door as Becky is closing it. It seems he must be a coward, and this is his way of impressing the hens. Today he miscalculated and landed outside the door. Brave rooster was happy to get back inside.

Christmas Letter, 2007: This year's leghorn pullets spent the summer outside in a moveable pen. Sam and Mary made the frame of the pen with PVC pipe and covered it with netting and tarp to keep the predators away and for protection from the rain. We moved the pen to fresh grass once or twice a day. We hoped they would peck the ground instead of each other. However, early this fall the hens began to peck the rooster so now they are wearing blinders.
    Last year we rescued two pecked hens and named them Henrietta and Henrianna. At night they slept in the greenhouse, but during the day they would wander around, busily scratching. They would come when the sheep were fed and eat any spilled grain. Mary said when they milked the cow near the woodshed, they had 14 sheep, one llama, 6 head of cattle, 2 chickens, and one dog hanging around.
    Last year's chickens laid a total of 4966 eggs.

Our Chickens

To the north of our house is a scenic point
    With a stream on either side,
And on this spot is a little house
    Where our happy hens abide.
They are pretty hens with bright red combs.
    Their feathers are long and white.
When all twenty-four line up on the floor,
    They are a beautiful sight.
Each morning I walk through the early dawn
    To give them fresh water to drink,
But Papa cleans out their house for me--
    I'm a lucky girl, I think.
The eggs that they lay for us to eat
    Are big and smooth and white.
I feed them two or three times a day,
    But I let them sleep all night.

                --Mary E. Miller

Excerpts from our Diary and Christmas Letters

Note: These entries tend to tell of bumper crops. The crops are not this abundant every year.

September 13, 1993--Monday: We dug the potatoes, washed them, and laid them on the race bank to dry. Papa said it made him think of "Potato Creek"! They yielded 39 bushels of good ones.

May 14, 1996--Tuesday: We planted 150 pounds of seed potatoes this afternoon. This evening we planted another row of strawberries. Last week we planted 17 rows of corn.

August 14, 1997--Thursday: We finished canning the green beans today with a total of 84 quarts. Last evening we gathered the first big amount of corn for the season. We didn't measure it, but we thought it might have been 20 bushels. Today we worked on the corn (between interruptions) until 9:15 P.M. We husked and brushed it, cooked it , and then cut it off the cob, but we did not finish boxing it.

August 15, 1997--Friday: Today we gathered 10 more bushels of corn and worked it up. Altogether we froze 100 quarts for us to use this winter, and then we froze some to give away. We also ate and gave away a number of ears of corn.

September 10, 1998--Thursday: We found a new way of pulling cucumber plants. Sam, Becky, and Mary started at one end and rolled the vines like a piece of carpet and then heaved them onto the trailer. Only a few scattered cucumbers remained.

June 14, 1999--Monday: This morning found us out in the berry patch again, and the weather was so pleasant that we could stay out until we were done. We picked 64 quarts. Sam claims that the berries ripen while we are picking! The cattle are right across the fence from the patch, and Zally, the calf, has discovered the bad berries we throw across the fence are quite tasty!

June 30, 1999--Wednesday: This evening we sped down the strawberry rows and picked less than a quart. We have picked 560 quarts of strawberries this season. We froze around 100 quarts of berries, made some jam, and had fresh strawberries every meal! We sold and gave berries away until Becky said she feels like we have plastered the town of Middlebury.

May 28, 2008--Wednesday There was a bit of frost this morning. After Becky had taken the newspapers off one row of beans, she noticed a small, nicely-shaped Indian arrowhead on the ground. A nice bonus for all the garden work she does!

STRAWBERRIES

The strawberry grows very close to the ground
  On a leafy and wide, sprawling vine.
And bending to pick all the juicy, red fruit
  Brings aches to this poor back of mine.
Sometimes I go down on my hands and my knees.
  It takes little thinking to guess
Just how my knees feel when I've crawled through the patch
  And the state of my poor, muddy dress.
And then the mosquitoes come swarming around.
  At ev'ry good chance they alight.
We wave and we swat and they still get their way.
  Oh, the sting and the itch of that bite!
Sometimes it's so cold that we shiver and fret.
  Sometimes it's midsummery hot.
"So why don't you give up the patch?" you may ask.
  I answer, "Most certainly not!"
Consider the tasty, delicious, good things
  The beautiful strawberries make.
How good they are, crushed, with vanilla ice cream
  On a piece of a white mountain cake!
The biscuity short cakes are very good, too,
  With fresh, golden butter they're spread,
Then strawberries, sugar, and milk go on top.
  And jam is delicious on bread.
And what a great treat are the cold, creamy shakes
  We drink on a hot summer day!
Next winter we'll eat of the strawberries which
  We are busily putting away.
Oh, yes, I'll good-naturedly grumble, I know,
  Of backaches, mosquitoes, and heat,
But I will endure them and plug down the row
  For I want good berries to eat!

--Mary Miller

Recipe for
Mixed Pickle

Each of the following vegetables should be cooked until nearly soft, then drained:
2 lb. navy beans
2 cups lima beans
4 cups small onions
2 cups diced carrots
1 stalk celery, diced
1 medium head cauliflower, cut into small pieces

Drain the following:
1 2-lb. can kidney beans
4 cups cooked corn

Wash and cut into small chunks:
2 red sweet peppers
2 green peppers
1 1/2 cups cucumbers
miniature cucumbers (optional)

Mix all the vegetables together and drain again. Pack loosely into jars. Add 1/2 teaspoon salt and 1/8 teaspoon celery seed per pint.
Boil the following ingredients together and pour over vegetables in jars:
4 cups sugar
4 cups vinegar
2 teaspoons turmeric
Process in boiling water bath for 30 minutes. Makes about 15 pints.

This is a recipe handed down from Grandma Miller. Our guests sometimes call it Last of the Garden or Chow Chow.

My Favorite Store

Oh, come with me early this morning
    For our food supply is low,
And I know a place that is open
    Whenever we care to go.

We do not have far to travel
    The fresh, cool air is a treat,
And music softly is playing
    In notes so cheery and sweet.

The displays of produce are lovely,
    Some corn on the ear we'll choose,
And such red, juicy tomatoes
    How could we ever refuse?

New potatoes make such good eating,
    So do the cukes crisp and green.
Let's pick out a fine muskmelon
    The ripest that can be seen.

Some onions would add good flavor
    There are plenty of them near,
Take this cabbage for a salad
    Plus these carrots over here.

Some little yellow ground cherries
    There are just enough for pie.
It's nearly time for us to leave
    For our "cart" is piled high.

We'll stop yet in the florist aisle
    What displays there are today!
Glads, phlox, and blue forget-me-nots
    We'll choose a nice bouquet.

And now this store has no checkout
    We may have it all for free,
For this little store's our garden
    And we've paid in work, you see.

But, wait, have we really earned it?
    We only planted the seeds,
And tended well the growing plants
    And hoed and pulled the weeds.

It is God Who sent the sunshine
    And He Who sent us the rain
'Tis He Who caused the plants to grow
    Without Him would be no gain.

So with thankful hearts to the Giver
    We walk back the homeward way,
And gladly prepare the bounty,
    That will fill our table today.
        Rebecca Miller

Recipe for
Hamburger and Potato Casserole

1 cup cream
10 cups cooked, grated potatoes
1 to 1 1/2 pounds hamburger
1/4 cup chopped onion
seasoned salt
1/4 to 1/2 pound processed cheese

Fry hamburger and onion together, adding 1/2 to 3/4 teaspoon salt. Pour cream into 4-qt. greased casserole. Alternate layers of potatoes, hamburger, seasoned salt (sprinkle to suit your taste), and cheese, making about 3 to 4 layers. Bake in oven until hot. Stir before serving.

Recipe for
Hamburger Steaks

2 pounds hamburger
1 1/3 cups cracker crumbs
2/3 cup cold water
Condensed cream of mushroom soup

Mix hamburger, cracker crumbs, and water together. Flatten in 9"x13" glass baking pan. Cut into 12 to 15 pieces and bake in 350° oven until centers of pieces are no longer pink (one hour or more.) Heat condensed cream of mushroom soup and spoon over tops of steaks before serving.
If you do not use the mushroom soup, stir in about 1/2 teaspoon salt with the meat mixture.

Of Thankfulness and Green Beans

We've grown green beans in our garden
    Each year since before I was born.
Green beans are okay, but my preference
    Has always been peas or sweet corn.

I learned peas were quite temperamental.
    If the weather was dry, they turned brown.
When summers were cool and cloudy,
    The yield from the sweet corn was down.

But beans--we had beans in abundance.
    We planted the seeds and they grew.
They matured and produced just like clockwork--
    The way I expected them to.

I was thankful each year for the sweet corn.
    I was glad for each bushel of peas.
But beans--why be thankful for something
    Which grew with such regular ease?

That is till one year when the bean crop
    Was actually meagerly poor.
Our friends kindly came to our rescue
    And gave all we needed and more.

I believe I have learned a good lesson
    Since the year when the crop was so lean,
For now I attach greater value
    To the plain and the humble green bean.

--Mary E. Miller

The Garden of My Heart

In the lovely springtime
  When we plant the seeds,
Soon begins the battle
  Of keeping down the weeds.

So with cultivator,
  And with swinging hoes,
Stooping now and weeding
  We go down the rows.

Never do our labors
  Find each single one.
Still it looks much better
  When our job is done!

Patient, constant labor
  Keeps weeds in control
So the final harvest
  May be bountiful.

Seedlings of bad habits
  Spring up ev'rywhere.
I must watch the garden
  Of my heart with prayer.

If I ask His pardon
  In sincerity,
If I plead for wisdom
  With humility,

God will surely help me
  Such weeds to uproot,
So the godly habits
  May bring forth more fruit.

If the Master Gardener
  Has complete control,
Surely then the harvest
  Will be bountiful.

    --Mary Miller

Chapter Six

WORK IN THE CIDER MILL

Customers waiting in line at the cider mill
Photo taken in 1953 when our grandparents lived here
Photo Courtesy of *The Elkhart Truth*

The Mill

In 1925, our Grandfather Miller bought what was known as the Lower Mill and ran a sawmill and a cider mill with the help of his sons. The sawmill was sold in 1944. In 1954, after most of his boys had left home, the cider mill equipment was also sold.

Our parents reopened the cider mill in 1977. Work in the mill starts in late summer with making peachbutter.

Around the first of September, we start making cider. We buy our apples. Several customers have allowed us to pick apples or peaches in their orchards. Our experiences there inspired Mary to write the orchard poems in this chapter. We sell cider retail and make cider for customers that bring their apples and want the cider for their own use. Because we do not pasteurize the cider, we can no longer sell it wholesale or make cider for people who sell it. This law went into effect in January of 2004.

As soon as the cider making slows down, we start making applebutter which is one of our specialties. Its sweetness comes only from the apples with which it is made.

We used to boil maple syrup in the spring, but we no longer do this since our father passed away. We now buy maple syrup from other producers to sell here.

The cider mill and old mill (which used to house the sawmill) both have turbine type waterwheels. The story goes that two men were involved in the building of the millrace and the original dam. One man dug the millrace with oxen and slip scraper while the other man built the dam. Both projects took about a year. Water rights for a hydraulic canal were obtained around 1850.

The water power is no longer used in the cider mill. We do use it in the old mill for cooling the apples and peaches, to irrigate our garden, and to power a few woodworking tools.

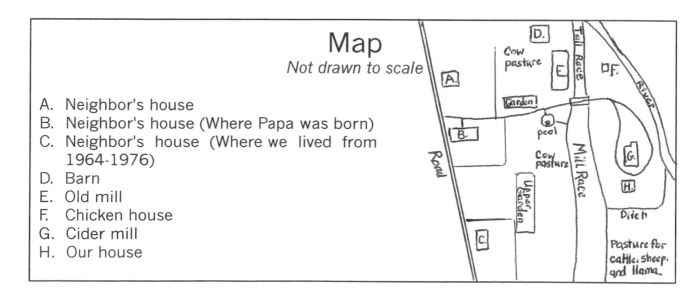

Map
Not drawn to scale

A. Neighbor's house
B. Neighbor's house (Where Papa was born)
C. Neighbor's house (Where we lived from 1964-1976)
D. Barn
E. Old mill
F. Chicken house
G. Cider mill
H. Our house

Out in the orchard where the apples grow
With a rich, red tint or golden glow,
With a rosy blush or maybe a stripe,
Out in the orchard when the apples are ripe.

Out in the orchard where the ground is spread
With a carpet of fruit from the limbs o'er head,
With apples on the trees and apples on the ground,
Out in the orchard there is fruit all around.

Out in the orchard where the branches up high
Hold strings of apples against the sky.
The blue and the gold and the leafy green--
Out in the orchard what a breath-taking scene!

Out in the orchard where the oak trees tall
Are framing the orchard with colors of fall.
And the yellow jackets dine with a sting and a hum.
Out in the orchard when autumn is come.

Out in the orchard where the crates fill up fast,
And the heart fills with mem'ries which by far will outlast
The sweet, crunchy apples and the bright days of fall.
Out in the orchard enjoy it all.

--Mary E. Miller

129

The Millers Mill
Middlebury, IN

The Cider Mill

When the trees are slowly changing
   to their brightly colored suits,
And the apple trees are loaded
   with their red and yellow fruits,
When the breezes hold a promise
   of the autumn's coming chill,
Then it's time to pay a visit
   to the busy cider mill.
See the great, green-roofed, white building,
   smell the apples, hear the din
Of the heavy thump, thump, thump, thump
   of the apples coming in.

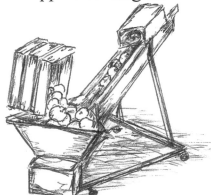

Down they roll into the building
   with a cheerful little dash,
And they drop into the water
   with a merry kind of splash.

Then the auger bears them upward
   where the growling grinder sits.
How it clatters as it batters
   all the apples into bits!

Watch the apple pieces fall
   into the hopper down below.
As more pieces tumble downward,
   see the mound inside it grow.

Near the press a pan is waiting
   lined with shiny stainless steel.
Notice how each corner of it
   boasts a sturdy iron wheel.
Since the pan is very heavy
   it is placed upon a track.
Later it will move upon this
   to the press and then come back.

Now two slats of heavy maple
   are laid flat upon the pan.
Next a frame is placed upon it,
   and a blanket stained deep tan
With a toss is thrown across it
   and positioned with swift care.
Are the edges somewhat even?
   Are the corners deep and square?

From the bottom of the hopper
   where the apple pieces fall
Runs a hose through which is carried
   apple pulp--seeds, stems, and all
To the pan. The hose is firmly
   held as back and forth it goes.
See how neatly ground-up apples
   lie in slightly mounded rows!

If the hopper runs too empty,
   how the pump can growl and cough!
When the cloth contains its quota,
   then the pump is switched to off.
Now the cloth is swiftly folded,
   frame is raised, and one more slat
Is slapped down, the frame is lowered,
   and a cloth is placed on that.
Care is taken so the blankets
   and the slats are placed on straight.
In this way the stack keeps growing
   till the blankets number eight,
Or until the batch of apples
   is exhausted, then it's done.
Thus, sometimes the cloths are fewer,
   sometimes there is only one.

Quiet reigns when pump and grinder
   and the auger are shut down.
Notice how the cloths are dripping
   drops of cider, tannish-brown.

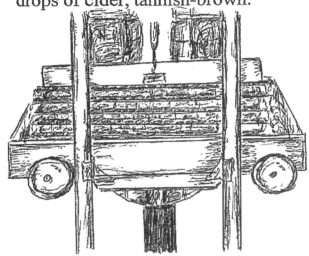

With a grunting shove and push
   the cart is rolled upon its track.
There! It's in the right position.
   Hear the throbbing noise out back.
That's the pump which pumps hydraulic
   oil that makes the press plate rise.
You can see its slow, slow motion
   if you watch with careful eyes.
Up, up goes the stack of blankets.
   How the streaming cider flows!
While another pump removes it
   through a one-inch plastic hose.

Want to try a cup of cider,
   fresh and cool and tangy-sweet?
Good! You like it! Many people
   like this special autumn treat.
Did you say you'll buy some cider
   so that you can drink your fill?
Here it is! And thanks for coming
   to the Miller's cider mill!
            --Mary E. Miller

Excerpts from our Diary and Christmas Letters

September 30, 1994—Friday: We have been busy making cider, especially on Tuesdays and Fridays. We have many nice and interesting customers. At the end of the day we have a lot to talk about. There is the man who brings us doughnuts quite often, the couple who says they consider coming to the mill their vacation, the "early birds" who try to get here first and have to come here earlier and earlier to make it, etc. The customers are often helping each other and visiting together. We girls put our names on our aprons because the customers have such a difficult time telling us apart. One time when Kathy and Mary were working in the mill, someone said to Mary, "I had to figure out if there are 2 of you girls working here or just one girl that is everywhere at once!"

September 18, 1998—Friday: We were busy making cider this morning. We girls sometimes sing while we are jugging, and one customer comes in and puts in the bass. We call ourselves the "Cidermill Quartet"!

January 22, 2004—Thursday: Orchard Hill Farms brought a load of apples this morning which we made into cider for applebutter. When Sam took a load of apple pulp to the pasture to dump, the wheel of the trailer broke through the frozen crust and in it sank. He unhitched the trailer and hitched it up again three times at different angles before he could get it out. Meanwhile, Papa and Kathy kept working in the cider mill. They dumped 8 blankets and sent the pulp outside as usual. When Sam returned with the tractor and trailer, there was a neat pile of apple pulp on the ground where the trailer belongs!

September 30, 2005—Friday: When Sam is busy, Mary takes the apple pulp to the pasture to dump. Today Bea and Vi, the sheep, got out when she opened the gate. However, they followed her right back through the gate. Then a lamb persisted in walking slowly in front of the tractor for several yards. The cattle and sheep were crowding up to the trailer, but she managed to back up and dump the pulp. She went back to make sure everyone was okay and saw a lamb lying down. It looked like Bonnie, the cow, was stepping on its leg. The lamb was not in distress but happily eating pulp. Mary grabbed a cornstalk and persuaded Bonnie to move, then prodded the lamb until she stood. The lamb got up and kept on eating! The animals seem to be addicted to the pulp.

October 21, 2005—Friday: We post the recipe for the cider on the cider tank for our customers to see. Today's batch was as follows: Macintosh—47%, Gala—20%, Red Delicious—8%, Yellow Delicious—8%, Grimes Golden—7%, Ida Red—5%, and Jonathan—5%.

A Fruitful Tree

And he shall be like a tree
planted by the rivers of water,
that bringeth forth his fruit in
his season; his leaf also shall
not wither; and whatsoever he
doeth shall prosper. Psalm 1:3

Lord, may I be a fruitful tree
  Beside the waters planted,
To which a green, unwithered leaf
  Unceasingly is granted.
Which is not careful in the drought,
  In heat has no despairing,
And in old age still knows the joy
  Of rich, productive bearing.

I praise Thee, Lord, for long ago
  Thou hearkened to my crying,
And plucked me from that evil root,
  And saved my soul from dying.
Thou grafted me into Thyself
  And granted me the pleasure
Of bearing precious fruit for Thee.
  This privilege I treasure.

Lord, grant to me a quiet strength
  Throughout each pruning season.
Thy love compels Thee thus to prune
  And always for this reason--
That I may bear abundant fruit.
  To yield is my decision.
So let this goal and not my pain
  Fill all my mind and vision.

Now may that fruit of righteousness,
  Love, peace, and holy gladness,
Be seen by weary passersby
  Whose hearts are full of sadness.
And may it teach them of Thy grace
  And Thy sweet invitation
To come to Thee and bear Thy fruit
  In joyful exultation.
                    Mary Elaine Miller

133

MAKING APPLEBUTTER

Yesterday we pressed the apples into cider sweet and brown.
Hear the old steam boiler running? Sam will cook the cider down.
See the pan here in the corner, rather long with rounding lid?
Down beneath the bubbling cider, steam-filled, one-inch pipes are hid.
There's a fan that blows the vapor through the vent and up the stack.
Let us go outside a moment through this way, now, there, step back.
Watch the cloud of steam that rises, white and puffy, proud and high,
Moving slowly, grandly upward in the blueness of the sky.
Now returning to the cider, it is briskly boiling well.
Ah! Inhale the sweet aroma. Don't you like the apple smell?
It will take about an hour
   till the present batch is done,
And the volume of the cider
   is reduced from six to one.
When the hydrometric reading
   in Baume is twenty-eight,
Sam will draw it off in buckets.
   That's the cider concentrate.

Now we're getting down to business. This is applebutter day.
Rinse the apples through the water. Watch for leaves to throw away.

First, two bushels of the Jonnies.
   Yes, that's right, we cook them whole.
Next five bushels Red Delicious,
   and the kettle's more than full.
Then the lid goes on the apples,
   carefully, so none will fall.
Now the steam will heat the kettle
   which is made with double wall.
As the apples cook and soften,
   they will occupy less space.
Then the lid will slowly settle
   to its old accustomed place.

Here's the applebutter kettle,
   also made of stainless steel.
One can tilt it back or forward
   if one turns this little wheel.
Into this is poured the cider.
   It can be such splashy stuff!
Seventeen and one-half gallons
   for one batch is quite enough.

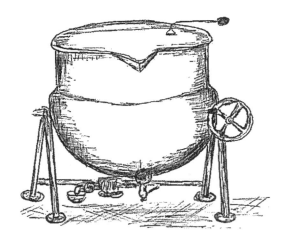

Now the apples are done cooking, soft and brown, yet still intact.
Here's the stick, and Sam is ready for the apple-stirring act.

Here's Victorio, the strainer,
   which we put the apples through.
With this small electric motor
   it won't take that long to do.
Down the trough into the kettle
   in an intermittent flow
Runs the sauce, and here's the bucket
   where the seeds and peelings go.
We must watch the sauce and cider as it comes up to a boil.
Quick! The frothy foam is rising! Calm it with a squirt of oil.
Yes, that's right, we add no sugar. All that cider makes it sweet.
It's a spread that diabetics can, in moderation, eat.
In an hour and a quarter, more or less, Sam says it's done.
See the stacks of jars awaiting? Watch us fill them one by one.
Here's the room where we will store it or display it till it's sold.
Thus the tale of applebutter at the Miller's Mill is told.

But the story hasn't ended
   for the folks who buy a bit,
For the most important process
   is the eating, isn't it?
                    --Mary E. Miller

Recipe for
Apple Crumb Pie

6 cups sliced Golden Delicious apples
1/2 cup sugar
1/3 cup flour
1 teaspoon cinnamon

Topping:
1/2 cup brown sugar
1/3 cup flour
3 tablespoons butter

Mix together sugar, flour, and cinnamon; stir in apples, and pour into 9-inch unbaked pie shell. Mix brown sugar and flour together; work in butter just until crumbly. Sprinkle crumbs on top of apples. Bake at 350°. The length of baking time seems to vary, but it is wise to allow 2 hours. It is done when apples feel soft when poked with a toothpick.

Recipe for
Mincemeat Pie

2 1/2 cups shredded raw apples
3/4 cup beef roast, cooked and ground
1/2 cup apple syrup
1/2 cup cooked raisins
1/2 teaspoon cinnamon
1/8 teaspoon allspice
1/8 teaspoon cloves

Mix together and pour into unbaked 9-inch pie shell. Top with pie crust. Bake at 350° until crust is nicely browned.

My mother revised this recipe of Grandma Miller's. (Grandma's version was much more indefinite.) The apple syrup (formerly called boiled cider) is apple cider concentrated to about one sixth of its original volume. See the poem "Making Applebutter" to see how it is made in our mill.

The Peach Orchard

The late-summer air is filled with the fragrance
   Of ripe, blushing peaches that hang from the tree
I reach up to pick them--My bucket's o'er flowing
   This late summer harvest is pleasant to see
The birds in their leisure are twittering gayly
   They sing of the broods that have taken to flight
The dome of the sky is as blue as a bluebird
   And o'er all the orchard lies sunshine so bright.
No hustle and bustle of traffic is heard here
   The cool morning wind gently rustles the leaves
It plays with the clover, the grass, and gold blossoms
   And the carpet of flowers growing under the trees.
Ah, peach-picking time to me is delightful!
   This peach in my hand is a beauty I see
I break it in half and I eat it with pleasure
   What good, juicy tidbits fresh peaches can be!
We fill up our bushels; we're done but we linger
   The air is so balmy, the place is so dear
We turn with reluctance and then journey homeward
   Good-bye, oh peach orchard, we'll see you next year.

                              --Mary E. Miller

Excerpt from our Christmas Letter

Christmas letter, 2002: Peachbutter season came early this year. On July 29, we received a call from an orchard in Michigan, saying they have small but nice Harrow Diamond peaches we could pick for a good price. We packed lunch and crates and left for the orchard. We found the picking to be very nice. We were especially grateful because peaches were scarce this year. We picked 72 bushels, and the next day we went back for 15 1/2 more, putting them into cold storage until we could use them.

To make the peachbutter, Papa dips a bushel of peaches into a kettle of hot water, then dumps them into cold water. This helps the skins slip off more easily. We sit around a table, peeling and pitting peaches and more peaches, around 15 bushels a morning. Sam puts them through a meat grinder. While we work, we sing, play games, or listen to stories on tapes.

The peaches cook while we eat dinner. Next the men add sugar and boil the peachbutter down to the right consistency, then put it into jars. A 15-bushel batch makes around 40 gallons. With all the canning and freezing we do during this time, peach season is often our busiest time of the year.

Post Peachbutter Days

The cleaning had been laid aside.
    The mowing had to wait.
And hoeing weeds had been postponed
    Until a later date.

We eat more cake and less of pie.
    We sometimes buy our bread.
We skimp on time-consuming foods
    And fix quick meals instead.

For there were peaches to be picked,
    Peachbutter to be made.
Now that is done and we must do
    The work that was delayed.

Besides all this we're freezing corn
    And canning peaches, too.
And other foods must be preserved.
    There's, oh, so much to do!

Be calm, my soul, amid your cares,
    And work with zeal and zest.
Think of the many hungry folks
    And count yourself well blest.

                    --Mary E. Miller

Excerpt from our Christmas Letter

Christmas letter, 1995: When is it time to begin tapping maple trees? That is a good question. Cousin Perry says to watch when the neighbors tap! The ideal weather is when the temperatures consistently dip below freezing at night and rise to 40-50 degrees during the day. If we tap too early, the holes will begin sealing over before the good runs come, but if we wait too long, we miss them.

This year we began tapping February 22. We tap trees along the road which often produce sweeter sap than trees in a woods. First Papa drills 1 to 3 tap holes in each hard maple tree, depending on its size. We girls place the buckets and lids beside the tree, and then Sam puts the spile in the tree and the hose in the bucket. A brick or stone is placed on each lid to help keep the bucket in place when the wild spring winds come.

After we are finished tapping, the men put the 300-gallon tank on the truck. By using the intake manifold on the truck to create vacuum, Sam can suck the sap from the buckets with a hose while we girls drive the truck. Sometimes the sap runs so well some of the buckets are overflowing before all the sap is gathered. Papa boils the sap in the cider mill. It takes 30-40 gallons of sap to make one gallon of syrup.

Maple syrup is very good on pancakes. We often serve syrup with homemade bread or dinner rolls to our company. Taffy is always a treat.

We bring in the buckets when the holes start to plug up or the sap gets cloudy. This year we gathered them in March 20. The land owners each get a share of syrup.

The season is quite enjoyable up until this point. But the syrup season is not over until the nearly 500 5-gallon buckets are washed and rinsed and stacked upstairs.

This year our maple syrup crop was down, and we also had difficulty finding syrup in Michigan to supplement our supply. Hopefully, next year will be a better year.

Note: Since Papa passed away in 2004, we have not been making maple syrup, but have been buying it to sell.

MAPLE SYRUP

Clear and amber,
  Sticky sweet.
Maple syrup!
  What a treat!
On our pancakes
  Or on bread,
With the melting
  Butter spread.
Or on biscuits
  Flaky, white,
Makes our oatmeal
  Taste just right.
What hard work
  And fun you bring,
Tasty harbinger
  Of spring!
    --Mary Miller

WORK

Our time is a gift from God,
  Our talents, and strength, and skill.
And have we not given ourselves
  To daily accomplish His will?
If, therefore, our time, and ourselves,
  Our strength, and the work are God's own,
And the wisdom of God far excels
  All wisdom that mankind has known,
Does not God have skill to direct
  His workers and work day by day
So what He requires may be done
  In a cheerful and Christian-like way?
However, experience would teach
  That many must sadly confess
Too often one's patience wears thin
  And tension mounts high under stress.
Lord, teach us to honestly look
  Each day to the truth of Thy Word.
Lord, grant that our hearts may be tuned
  That Thy Spirit's small voice may be heard,
So we may know how to avoid
  Ambitions encouraged by pride.
Unselfish impulses will rule
  If Thou art our Master and Guide.
Oh, how it relieves stress and strain
  To work not for praise or reward,
But doing what needs to be done
  With heartiness as to the Lord!
What comfort to know that our God
  Requires no more than one's best.
His children who give this to Him
  Can trust Him to care for the rest!

--Mary Miller

Chapter Seven

VERSES FOR
GREETING CARDS

A homemade greeting card
with a windmill made of toothpicks

Making Greeting Cards

One day Mama announced that buying cards was getting too expensive. She said that she was going to make cards and we girls could help her.

We sat around the dining room table, and she had us cut out pictures. She took 8 1/2" x 11" typing papers and folded them carefully into fourths. We pasted the pretty pictures from old cards or perhaps seed catalogs onto the cards, and Mama wrote in the messages. We were quite small, and Kathy's and my own attempts were rather pathetic. Mary probably was just a baby so, of course, she did not help. This is the way I remember our card-making venture began.

As we grew older, our greeting cards did improve. Sometimes they became rather elaborate. It was an excellent way to improve our artistic abilities. Before long we began hearing people say they like homemade cards better than boughten ones. They would often tell us how they saved our cards and how much they meant to them. It was a surprising response to a project we had begun only to save money. We have found that making computer cards better fits our busy schedule, but the practice those handmade ones gave us is still helpful.

Eventually Mary penned verses for the inside of our cards. We have collected many of those verses for this chapter. We have also included directions for making a number of homemade greeting cards. Of course, the verses can be used for other kinds of homemade cards or in letters, etc.

E. Ruth Miller

Tips for Making Homemade Cards:

Unless card size is specifically mentioned, the cards in this chapter are made using an 8 1/2" x 5 1/2" piece of heavy-weight paper folded in half. Larger papers would also work for most of these.

Check with the office supplies for envelopes and heavy-weight paper.

Happy Birthday! *Poems for Birthday Cards*

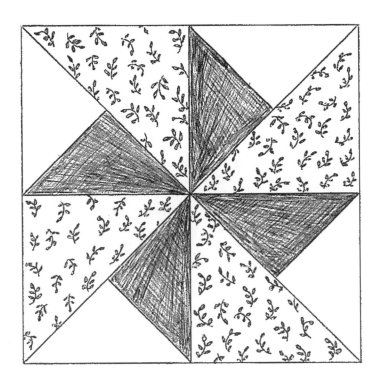

Using the bits and the pieces
    Gathered from here and from there,
Taking much thought in designing
    Each diamond, triangle, and square.
Those who have skill, time, and patience
    To bring to an end such a feat
Can make of those bits and those pieces
    A quilt that is whole and complete.
Look back on the year that has ended
    And carefully, fondly review
The kindnesses, love, and affection
    Which others have showered on you.
Take highlights from happy occasions,
    And joys that are common each day,
And the good that you learned from the trials
    Which now and then clouded your way.
Put all of this brightness together,
    Be thankful for every part,
And you'll have a beautiful patchwork
    Of memories stored in your heart.
                M.E.M.

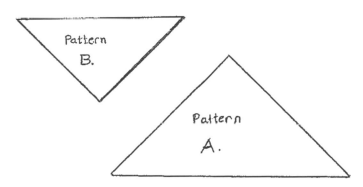

Since birthday gifts traditional
    This year are very few,
You'll have to take our word for it,
    And trust that word is true,
How very deep and tender is
    The love we have for you!
                M.E.M.

How to Make a Quilt Block Card:
Make patterns A and B.
You will need three different colors (or shades of colors) of paper for the quilt block. You may want to use wrapping paper with a small design for one or two of the colors.
Using pattern A, cut out 4 of color #1.
Using pattern B, cut out 4 of color #2, and 4 of color #3.
Lay the pieces out to make the quilt block.
Carefully paste onto the front of the card.

It's good on one's birthday
    One's blessings to count.
There's always a cheering,
    Amazing amount.
And now on your birthday
    We think of ours, too--
The blessing of sharing
    A friendship with you.
                M.E.M.

These flowers drank in the raindrops
That fell through the summer days.
With pleasure they lifted their faces
To the warmth of the sun's bright rays.
Though now their days in the garden
Have slipped away and gone,
Their beauty which gave such pleasure
Is lingering steadily on.
On your birthday collect ev'ry brightness
And do not let them depart,
But press those wonderful mem'ries
On the pages of your heart!
M.E.M.

How to Make Greeting Cards with Pressed Flowers:
(If you need directions for pressing flowers, look up *How to Press Flowers* in the index.)
Select pressed flower(s) and arrange on the front of the card. A tweezers may be used for small and fragile flowers.
Cut a piece of adhesive transparent paper <u>larger</u> than the front of the card.
Peel off paper backing and place transparent adhesive over the flowers. This can be <u>very</u> tricky if the arrangement is complicated because the flowers move toward the adhesive. (It helps to have two people doing it so that each corner can be held while putting it on quickly.) Press down smoothly.
Trim excess transparent adhesive from edges of the card.

May your birthday be filled to o'erflowing
With happiness, joyfully knowing
That you have been thought of
with warmth and with cheer
And enough pleasant wishes to last through the year.
M.E.M.

Beautiful moments, splendid new things,
Happy, long-waited-for happenings,
Trustful contentment all the year through--
These are the blessings we're wishing for you!
M.E.M.

1.

2.

3.

4.

How to Make a Windmill Card with Toothpicks:

   You can put the windmill on the front of a plain card or cut out a scenic picture from a magazine or calendar and use that for a background. You may want to find a picture to go with the poem you choose.

You will need about 15 flat toothpicks.

Put some white multi-purpose glue onto a scrap of paper. Dip your finger into the glue and coat the backside of the toothpicks when glueing them into place.

1. Start with two full-length toothpicks. With the narrow ends at the top, make an upside down V.

2. Cut a dozen or so toothpicks in half with a scissors. Use the more narrow halves for the blades, pasting the smaller ends in the center of the wheel.

3. Fit 3 small pieces of toothpicks in the upside down V.

4. Cut 2 more small pieces and slant them between the 3 small pieces. (See diagram.)

What shall I wish for your birthday
   And also the rest of the year,
Only those things which are pleasant,
   Sunshine from skies blue and clear?
I'll wish such, but since we both realize
   At times storms will come to us all,
I'll wish that with gentle refreshment
   The showers upon you may fall.
And after the rainstorm is over,
   When clouds have begun to depart,
I'll wish you the loveliest rainbow
   That ever took place in your heart!
                M.E.M.

Some evenings when the setting sun
   Has vanished from our sight,
There lingers in the western sky
   An afterglow of light.

May gladness fill your birthday now,
   And when the day is gone,
May mem'ry find an afterglow
   Of pleasure ling'ring on.
             M.E.M.

A Birthday Prayer
Today I think upon the year
    Which has so quickly slipped away.
Forgive each error and mistake,
    And bless my efforts, Lord, I pray.
As day by day my new year comes
    Still may Thy Spirit ever be
Transforming me from what I am
    Into a person more like Thee!
M.E.M.

How to Make a Flower Holder for Poem:
Write or type the poem onto a piece of paper. Cut
the paper down to a small rectangle. Paste a piece
of dark blue construction paper behind it and trim it,
leaving about 1/8" border around the poem.
Trace the row of morning glories onto the front of a
card. (The card can be made with an 8 1/2" x 11"
regular-weight [copy] paper folded in fourths.) Color
the flowers blue and their centers yellow. Color the
leaves.
Carefully cut along the top edge of the flowers.
Make the slit long enough to hold the poem.
Tuck the poem into place and glue.

Friendship
Friendship is a precious thing
    To value and to treasure.
How good it is that friends can share
    The times of pain and pleasure!
And birthdays are a golden time
    For your friends to remind you
That friendship's warm and loving ties
    Continue still to bind you.
M.E.M.

Though even on your special day
    Our hearts in shadows lie,
We know that God directs the clouds
    Which sweep across the sky.
If He so wills, His hand can make
    A rainbow to appear,
And melting clouds will leave to us
    A sunny sky and clear.
But if God's love does not command
    The storm clouds to depart,
His glorious peace can shed a ray
    In ev'ry troubled heart.
How good it is to trust to Him
    A future so unsure,
And God Himself will go with us
    Throughout the coming year!
M.E.M.

Page One

HAD TO RUSH AROUND A BIT
WITH THIS "HAPPY BIRTHDAY" RHYME.

Page Two

HAD NO MOMENTS LEFT TO SPARE.

Page Three

MADE IT IN THE NICK OF TIME!

page 1.

page 2.

page 3.

How to Make a Cottontail Rabbit Card:
Use an 8 1/2 " x 11" piece of heavy weight paper such as card stock for the card. Fold into thirds. (See diagram.)
Trace the rabbits onto regular weight paper and cut them out. (Do not trace the tail.) You may want to color the rabbits and paste them into place. Or you may want to use them for patterns and cut them out of construction paper. (See diagram.)
Use a little piece of cotton for each tail.

Belated birthday wishes!
   This card has come to show
That we have not forgotten it
   Although we're very slow.
And though we missed your birthday,
   We still can wish you cheer
And peace and joy and happiness
   Each day, each week, all year!
                              M.E.M.

To try to make your birthday card
Arrive on schedule would be hard,
For we don't even know the date.
This may be early--may be late.
Although we've made a random guess,
The wishes for your happiness
Each day throughout the coming year
Are warm and friendly and sincere.
                              M.E.M.

Front of Card

An Evening Primrose

A bit of a movement, a twirl, and a shake,
The primrose was sleeping but now it's awake!
And now at your birthday a new year unfolds,
And moment by moment you'll find what it holds...

Inside of Card

...We wish you the best day by day. When it's through,
We hope you can say 'twas a good year for you!
M.E.M.

PATTERN C.

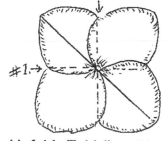

How to Make a Folding Primrose Card:

Use heavy-weight paper for the card such as card stock or poster board.

1. For the <u>front</u> of the card make patterns A and B. Trace around patterns onto yellow construction paper. Paste bud onto front of card. Draw a green stem with a felt-tip marker. (See above diagrams.)

2. For the <u>inside</u> of the card, make pattern C. and trace around the pattern onto yellow construction paper. Outline the flower with a yellow felt-tip marker or crayon. Use a brown felt-tip marker for the very center.

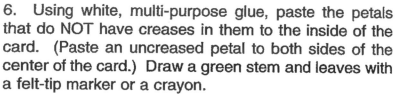

3. Fold flower in half along the dotted line with the right side facing out.

4. Unfold. Fold line #1 with the right side facing in. Unfold. Fold line #2 with the right side facing in.

5. Fold the flower together keeping the creases the way they already were folded. (Right side will be facing in.)

6. Using white, multi-purpose glue, paste the petals that do NOT have creases in them to the inside of the card. (Paste an uncreased petal to both sides of the center of the card.) Draw a green stem and leaves with a felt-tip marker or a crayon.

You may want to look up the JULY poem in the index to find sketches of an evening primrose opening up.

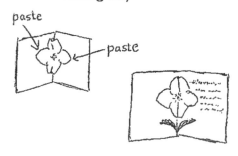

The seasons come and the seasons go;
The summer's green yields
to the winter's white snow.
And we are amazed as the seasons go by
How quickly, so swiftly, the passing years fly!
But one good thing the changing years do--
They give us the pleasure of saying to you,
"HAPPY BIRTHDAY!"
M.E.M.

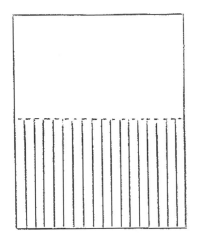

How to Make a Woven Card:

Choose two colors of construction paper that go well with each other such as yellow and brown, light blue and dark blue, or red and white. Fold the one 9" x 12" sheet in half. (If the piece is not quite 9", cut it to 8 1/2".

1. Measure and draw lines half an inch apart all the way across the one half. Cut on the lines from the bottom of the sheet to the fold.

2. Take the contrasting color and cut 12 strips 1/2" x 9". Weave one of these strips through the card. Slide the strip up tightly against the fold. Glue both ends of the strip into place.

3. Take another strip and weave it into the card. Slide it against the previous strip and glue both ends.

Continue weaving strips and gluing the ends until the card is full. You will probably have at least one extra strip. Glue the ends of the card to the last strip. Trim the bottom of both the back and front of the card even with the last strip. Trim the sides to make them even. You may turn the card so it opens on the side.

Decorate by pasting stickers and/or pictures onto it. For the poem about the seasons, you may want to cut small pictures out of an old calendar, one for each of the four seasons.

The changing years which change us all
    Have touched each life and heart and mind
With changes great or changes small,
    With painful change or changes kind.
To friendships dear which warm our hearts
    We hope each changing year may bring
The kind of change which love imparts--
    A beautifying strengthening.
                    M.E.M.

Twelve Days of Birthday!

Although we know this cake is fake.
We hope each love-filled piece will make
You feel the joy with which we send
Each birthday gift to you, dear friend!

M.E.M.

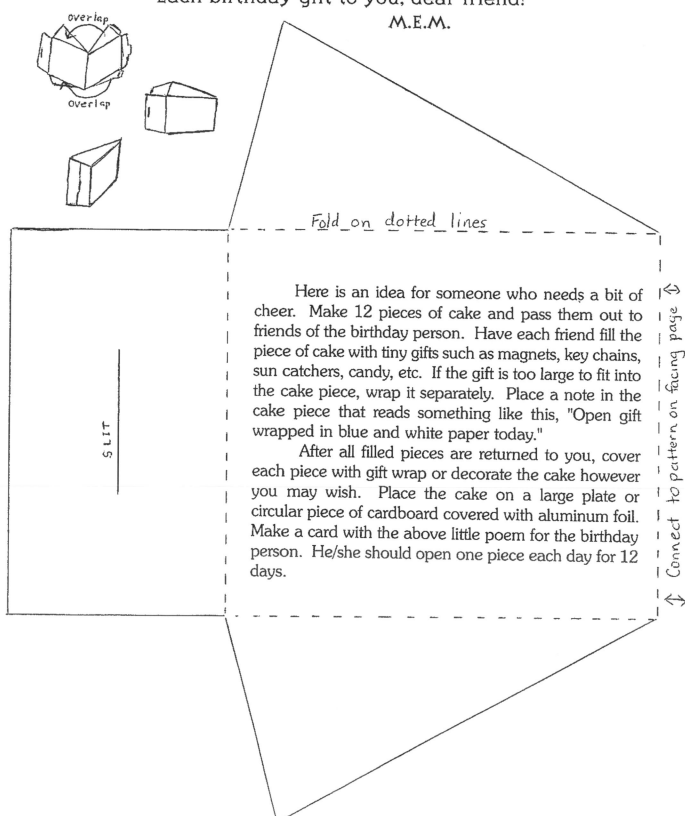

Fold on dotted lines

Here is an idea for someone who needs a bit of cheer. Make 12 pieces of cake and pass them out to friends of the birthday person. Have each friend fill the piece of cake with tiny gifts such as magnets, key chains, sun catchers, candy, etc. If the gift is too large to fit into the cake piece, wrap it separately. Place a note in the cake piece that reads something like this, "Open gift wrapped in blue and white paper today."

After all filled pieces are returned to you, cover each piece with gift wrap or decorate the cake however you may wish. Place the cake on a large plate or circular piece of cardboard covered with aluminum foil. Make a card with the above little poem for the birthday person. He/she should open one piece each day for 12 days.

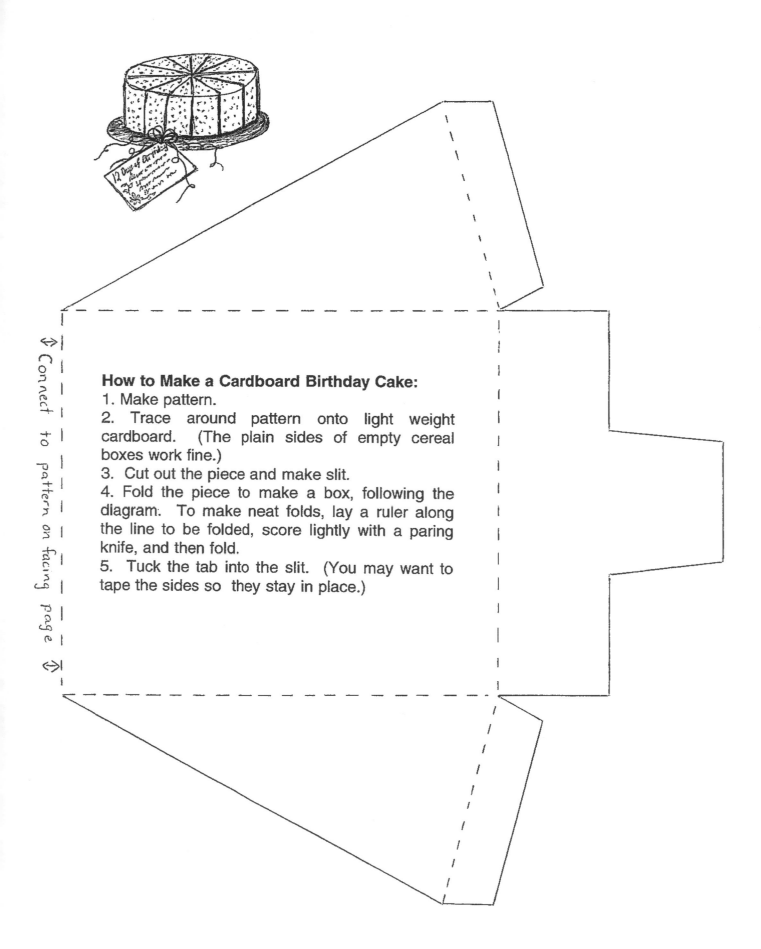

Connect to pattern on facing page ⇕

How to Make a Cardboard Birthday Cake:
1. Make pattern.
2. Trace around pattern onto light weight cardboard. (The plain sides of empty cereal boxes work fine.)
3. Cut out the piece and make slit.
4. Fold the piece to make a box, following the diagram. To make neat folds, lay a ruler along the line to be folded, score lightly with a paring knife, and then fold.
5. Tuck the tab into the slit. (You may want to tape the sides so they stay in place.)

Get Well Soon!
Poems for Get-Well and Thinking-of-You Cards

Page One
There isn't much that we can do
To ease the heaviness for you,
To lessen any pain you feel,
To make anxiety less real.
But, like a pansy's upturned face
Discovered in a lonely place,

Page Two
Like melodies of bird's sweet song
When winter has seemed cold and long,

Page Three
We hope the knowledge that we care
And oft remember you in prayer,
Like sunbeams from a cloud-filled dawn
Will touch your heart and cheer you on!
M.E.M.

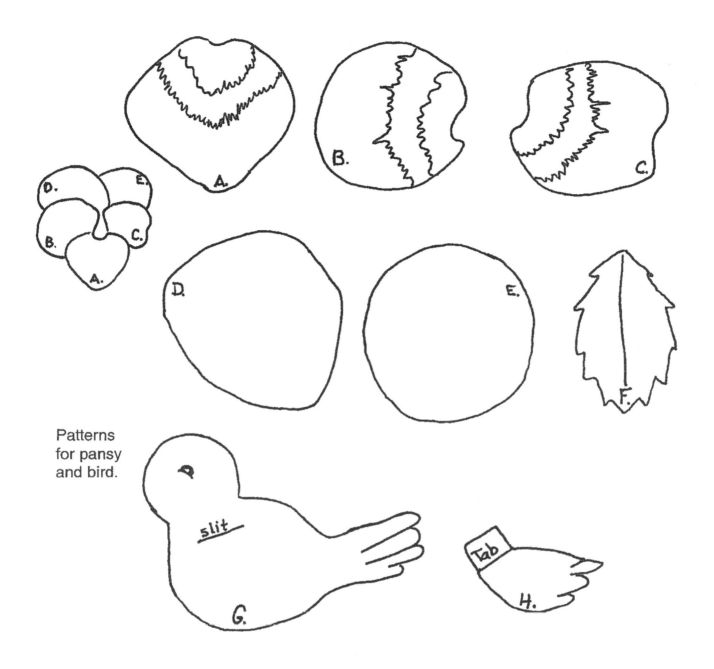

Patterns for pansy and bird.

How to Make a Pansy and Bird Card:

Fold an 8 1/2" x 11" sheet of heavy-weght paper into thirds for the card.

Make patterns.

Draw and cut around patterns A, B, and C, using light orange construction paper. Use dark orange construction paper for D and E. Outline with a brown or black felt tip marker. Cut 2 leaves (pattern F) from green construction paper. Arrange carefully onto the first page of the card, gluing into place.

Draw and cut around bird patterns G and H, using light blue construction paper. Slit an opening for the wing and slide the wing tab into the slit. Glue the bird into place on the second page. Do not glue the wing down, only its tab. Draw an eye with black felt tip marker and the beak and feet with orange felt tip marker. Draw music notes above the beak.

Variations: You may make the pansy a different color such as lavender and purple or light and dark blue.

155

How to Make Button Flowers and Birds:

Use heavy weight paper for the card, such as card stock or construction paper.

From your collection of used buttons, choose some brightly colored ones for the flowers. Outline and color the flowers with a felt-tip marker or pencil crayon the same color as the button. (Or you may want to use a brown or black button for the center of the flower and draw the petals a bright color.) Draw green stems and leaves.

To make a bird, choose a small and large button the same color (such as blue ones for a bluebird or yellow ones for a canary) then draw the tail using the same color. Draw an orange beak.

Fasten the button to the card with multi-purpose white glue. If you sew the button on with a couple strands of thread, it holds it in place better and adds to the effect.

[Please be careful to keep the buttons out the reach of children who might swallow them.]

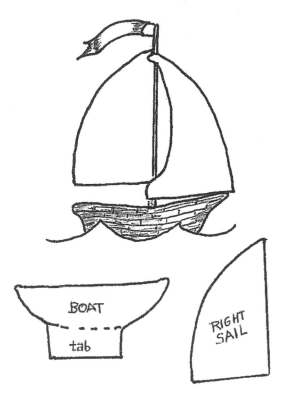

To tell you how it made us sad
   To hear that you were ailing.
Now may the way to better health
   Be smooth and easy sailing.
In fact, we hope you feel so well
   This card will seem belated,
But there is something we can say
   Which never is outdated.
We're glad to count you as our friend.
   Our best goes with you surely,
So press that thought upon your mind
   And hold it there securely.
                    M.E.M.

BOAT
tab

RIGHT SAIL

LEFT SAIL

FLAG

Glue underneath dots.

How to Make a Sailboat for a Card:

Use light blue construction paper for the card.

Draw a line of waves with a dark blue, felt-tip marker, about an inch from the bottom of the card.

Cut a slit along the wave.

Trace or copy patterns and cut them out.

Trace around boat pattern onto brown construction paper. Cut it out and tuck the bottom of the boat under the wave and glue the tab to hold it in place.

Tuck a flat toothpick (wider end) into the boat and glue the toothpick in place with white multi-purpose glue. Glue both tips of the boats sides to the card.

Cut sails out of white paper. Glue the right sail into place, gluing down only its points. Glue the left sail into place, covering half the tooth pick. Glue only what rests on the tooth pick and the bottom left point. (By not gluing the sails and boat flat against the card, it gives more of a 3-dimensional appearance.)

Cut out a red flag and glue into place. Draw 2 short lines with a black pen to connect the flag to the tooth pick.

_____(Name of person)*___, we hope you soon will be
Sailing toward recovery,
Trusting in our God Who cares,
Buoyed up by many pray'rs.
Thankful for each friend's concern,
Patient for good health's return,
Knowing that when storms are gone,
Rainbow hues will sparkle on.
                    M.E.M.

*"How we hope you soon will be" may be used instead of the name.

WE HOPE AND PRAY
   THAT YOURS WILL BE
A QUICK AND FULL
   RECOVERY!
                    M.E.M.

Dear Doctor, I'm hoping
   You'll soon feel just fine,
Not only for your sake--
   But also for mine!
                    M.E.M.

157

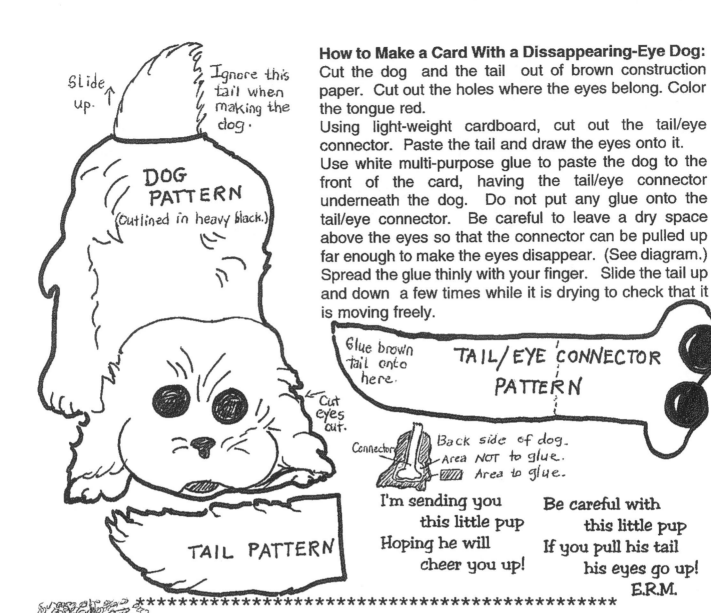

How to Make a Card With a Dissappearing-Eye Dog:

Cut the dog and the tail out of brown construction paper. Cut out the holes where the eyes belong. Color the tongue red.

Using light-weight cardboard, cut out the tail/eye connector. Paste the tail and draw the eyes onto it.

Use white multi-purpose glue to paste the dog to the front of the card, having the tail/eye connector underneath the dog. Do not put any glue onto the tail/eye connector. Be careful to leave a dry space above the eyes so that the connector can be pulled up far enough to make the eyes disappear. (See diagram.) Spread the glue thinly with your finger. Slide the tail up and down a few times while it is drying to check that it is moving freely.

Slide up.

Ignore this tail when making the dog.

DOG PATTERN
(Outlined in heavy black.)

Glue brown tail onto here.

TAIL/EYE CONNECTOR PATTERN

Cut eyes out.

Connector

Back side of dog.
Area NOT to glue.
Area to glue.

TAIL PATTERN

I'm sending you
  this little pup
Hoping he will
  cheer you up!

Be careful with
  this little pup
If you pull his tail
  his eyes go up!
      E.R.M.

****

You recall the hours of pleasure
You enjoyed so long ago,
Playing on the swing each summer,
Flying high, then swinging low.

If your swinging days are over,
Let this mem'ry make you smile.
Just relax in your recliner,
And pretend to swing a while!
HAVE A GOOD DAY!
      M.E.M.

How to Make a Card with a Swing:

Find an old calendar picture of a large tree. The tree should have a limb from which a swing can hang. Cut a flat toothpick (wider end) to about 1" long.

Using a heavy string (such as #10 crochet thread or kite string) double knot the string to the one end of the tooth pick. Tie the knot tightly. With a large needle, sew the other end of the string around the limb. Make sure it looks as though the swing is not far from the ground. Cut the string and tape it down on the backside of the picture. Repeat stringing process for the other end of the swing

Paste picture to the front of a card. You may want to glue the swing in place or let it swing.

158

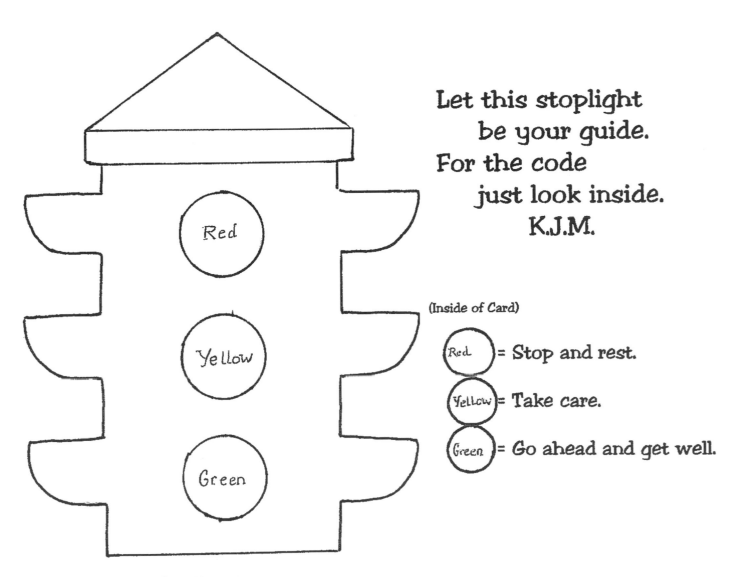

Let this stoplight
be your guide.
For the code
just look inside.
K.J.M.

(Inside of Card)

Red = Stop and rest.

Yellow = Take care.

Green = Go ahead and get well.

How to make a Stoplight Card:
Cut a stoplight out of orange construction paper. Cut out the holes.
Put a piece of the correct color of construction paper underneath each of the three holes: top hole--red, middle hole--yellow, bottom hole--green. Glue into place on the front of the card.
For the code on the inside of the card, cut out small circles or rectangles of the coinciding colors.

As the little hummingbird
Gathers sweetness from
each flower,
So may you, as faithfully,
Gather brightness from each hour.
Let the mem'ry of dull moments
Fade as soon as they are gone,
But resolve to let the brightness
Of the glad ones linger on.
M.E.M.

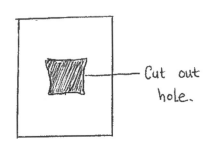

Cut out hole.

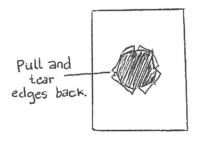

Pull and tear edges back.

We hope your operation
　　Will prove to be successful
And your recuperation
　　Won't prove to be too stressful.
We hope you have an antidote
　　For ev'ry hurting pain
And patience for each passing day
　　Until you're well again.
　　　　　　　　M.E.M.

I wish you the best
Of results from each test,
　　And calmness of heart while you wait,
And then may a wealth
Of excellent health
　　Return till you're feeling just great!
　　　　　　　M.E.M.

Since the day that I learned
That your cancer returned,
　　I have thought of you often, my friend.
Be assured that I care,
And many a pray'r
　　For you from my heart will ascend.
　　　　　　　M.E.M.

How to Make a Peep-Hole Card:
Use a calendar picture cut to cover the front of the card. Cut a somewhat square hole in the center. Pull and tear the edges back a little, making the opening more rounding. Fold the edges open. Color the folded edges black with a felt-tip permanent marker. Glue the edges down. Find a picture that looks nice behind the peep hole. (Suggestions: A sea gull behind a picture of a rocky coast, a deer behind a picture of a forest, etc.) Glue the pictures into place.

May you feel God's presence
    For He truly is there.
Be assured that His ear
    Hears every prayer.
His eye watches tenderly
    While awake or asleep.
The words He has spoken
    Are promises He'll keep.
His arm is much stronger
    Than what man can tell.
With Him on your side--
    ALL WILL BE WELL.
            E.R.M.

We pray for a miracle--
    His divine, healing touch,
For healing is something
    We want very much.
We pray that His will
    Be done in all things.
We pray that He'll keep you
    Under His wings.
May our faith grow strong.
    Lord, help all to see
Strength for each moment
    By looking to Thee.
            E.R.M.

If ev'ry thought of you would end in visits
    Or cheery notes expressing best regards,
You'd often find me waiting on the doorstep,
    And you would have a growing stack of cards.
Though only rarely do I write a letter,
    Or call on you to let you know I care,
Yet day by day a thought goes winging upward.
    I bring your name before God's throne in pray'r.
            M.E.M.

How to Add Detail to a Calendar Picture:
You can add an extra touch to a calendar picture by pasting a picture of an object or a sticker onto it. You can find objects to cut from calendars, old greeting cards, and flower and seed catalogs These are some suggestions:
    --Flying ducks above a picture of a lake.
    --Sea shells on a sea shore.
    --A bird sitting on its nest with trees in the background.
    --A mother hen in front of a farm scene.
Lay the object(s) on different pictures to see what looks best and where to place the object before deciding what to do. The results will likely surprise you.

Congratulations to the Graduate!

Poems for Graduation Cards

To the Graduate

Another learning goal attained.
Another milestone fairly gained.
Now pause a bit to
think and rest.
Relive the good of days gone by,
Then to the future cast your eye,
And know we wish you
all the best!

M.E.M.

To friends we know not half so well
We give a smile and simply tell
Them that we wish them happiness,
Bright dreams fulfilled, and life's success,
But you are dearer to our hearts.
The very best this world imparts
Is not enough to wish for you.
May joy and peace, unfeigned and true,
The kind which God alone can give
To those who choose for Him to live
Be yours to keep you safe and strong.
May God's word show you right from wrong.
And may you find that on life's way
You grow more like Him day by day.
For truly he is richly blessed
Who seeks not earth's, but heaven's best.

M.E.M.

May the future be bright with the promises
Of a splendid work to do,
Of plans to form, of goals to make,
And a purpose to pursue.
May disappointments only make
Your character grow strong.
May love and peace and inner joy
Be yours your whole life long.

M.E.M.

How to Make an Offset for a Picture:

Choose a calendar picture suitable for the front of the card you are making. Suggestions for a graduation card are a soaring bird, an open road or path, a schoolhouse, a mountain peak, etc. Cut the picture at least one inch smaller than the front of the card so when you center it onto the card, there will be a half inch (or more) margin all the way around.

Choose a color of construction paper that blends or contrasts well with the calendar picture. Cut the construction paper to the same size as the calendar picture.

Lay the picture in the center of the card. Put the piece of construction paper behind the picture and tilt it to an angle that looks nice. Glue into place.

Best Wishes for the Marriage

Poems for a Wedding Card and an Engagement Card

CHARITY

Charity suffereth long,
and is kind;
charity envieth not;
charity vaunteth not itself,
is not puffed up,
Doth not behave itself unseemly,
seeketh not her own,
is not easily provoked,
thinketh no evil;
Rejoiceth not in iniquity,
but rejoiceth in the truth;
Beareth all things,
believeth all things,
hopeth all things,
endureth all things.
I Corinthians 13: 4-7

When the solemn vows are spoken,
And the marriage has begun;
The happy hearts united--
No longer two, but one.
May the happy times bring courage,
Your hearts be filled with song;
May the times of care and trouble
Make your love and marriage strong.
May God be always near you
As you journey on through life.
Sincere congratulations
To a happy man and wife!

How to Make a Card

Fastened with a Ribbon:

Cut a sheet of white card stock paper down to 7" x 10". Fold in half.

1. Copy I Corinthians 13:4-7 onto a white or light blue paper. Cut the paper to size 4" x 6", leaving a space underneath the verses for a flower sticker. Cut a piece of blue construction paper to 4 1/2" x 6 1/2". Center the verses onto the construction paper and paste with glue stick. Center the construction paper onto the front of the card and glue into place.

2. For the inside of the card, copy the wedding poem onto a light blue sheet of regular weight paper. Cut slightly smaller than 10" x 7" and fold in half.

3. Place the poem sheet inside the card. Holding it in place, carefully punch a hole at the top and bottom of the card along the fold. Reach in as far as you can with a paper punch to make the holes.

4. Thread a blue, medium width ribbon through the holes. Tie a bow on the outside.

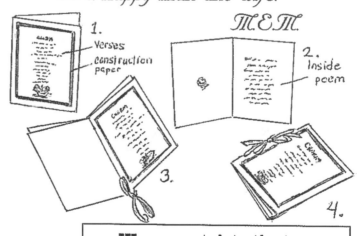

We congratulate the two
Soon to say the words,
"I do!"
God grant
patience as you wait
For your happy
wedding date.
And we pray
that He will bless
Both of you with happiness!
M.E.M.

On Your Anniversary

Poems for Anniversay Cards

Outside of card. Fold roses in.

diagram #1.

Happy Anniversary!

diagram #2.

Note: The 70th anniversary poem was written for a couple in their 90's. The husband liked to say, "Love is the glue that holds us together!"

How to Make a Double Rose Card:

Use heavy weight paper such as card stock for the card.

Trace the outline of the three sections of the card connecting "A" to "A" and "B" to "B." (See diagram #1.)

You may want to trace the roses onto regular weight paper, then cut them out and paste them onto the card. Or you may want to copy the roses directly onto the card.

Color the roses.

Fold the roses in to overlap each other. (See diagram #2.)

Note: The poems on the facing page can be changed to make them fit other anniversaries.

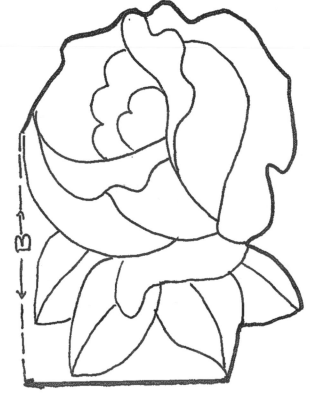

Only a sprouting seedling,
Only a budding flow'r,
Love showed a tender promise
In its unfolding hour.
Warmed by the happy moments,
Watered by sorrow's tears,
Love grew each day and flourished
Through all of these many years.
Treasure each day together
Loving and warm and true.
Long may love's solemn blessings
Be shed on both of you!
                    M.E.M.

The years have quietly slipped away,
Sixty of them, since your wedding day.
May ev'ry good day be a good one and plus,
As special to you as you've been to us!
                    M.E.M.

Through seventy years, no matter what came,
   Through sunshine or stormier weather,
Love was the glue that held you two
   And kept you both together.
So now we wish to congratulate
   A couple whose love is true.
Our wish for today and in days to come--
   The best of life's blessings to you!
                    M.E.M.

"Together" is a lovely word.
   It has a friendly sound,
And after sixty years of it
   What memories abound!

Through health and illness, joy and tears,
   Through fair and stormy weather,
You traveled through the days of life
   For sixty years--together.
                    M.E.M.

Your treasure chest of memories
   contains a liberal store
Of happy times throughout the years,
   now numbering forty-four.
Now may each passing day contain
   a jewel or a gem,
Until your hearts are simply full
   and overwhelmed with them!
                    M.E.M.

You haven't a need of this card to remind you
   Of the special occasion today we are sure,
For you've been reliving the day of your wedding
   Rememb'ring how happy the two of you were.
We congratulate you on the years spent together.
   We're hoping that you will enjoy many more.
May the year that awaits you be blessed and happy--
   More joyful than any experienced before!
                    M.E.M.

165

How to Make a Greeting Card Frame:

Use an 8 1/2" x 11" regular weight (copy) paper and type or copy the poem onto the bottom half of the page.

Fold the paper in half with poem exposed. Fold in half again, having the poem on the inside.

Trace the frame onto the front and cut out the hole, cutting only one thickness of paper. Color the flowers.

Tuck a picture of the couple's house or a house from a magazine behind the frame and carefully glue into place.

Note: The wording can be changed in the title to fit other anniversaries. In the fifth verse it can be made to say "many years" instead of "forty years."

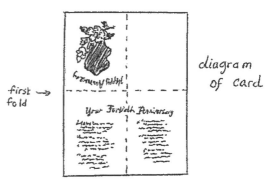

first → fold

diagram of card

Your Fortieth Anniversary

A time for happy memories
   And lingering reflection
Upon the years you two have lived
   With love and true affection.

A time for thankfulness to God,
   Deep gratitude expressing
For ev'ry kindness He has shown,
   His guidance, care, and blessing.

A time to look with confidence
   Upon the future, knowing
His kindnesses, as in the past,
   He will continue showing.

A time for us to thank you for
   The home which you established,
A home where love and kind regard
   Upon each one are lavished.

A time for us to give to you
   Sincere congratulations
For sharing forty years of all
   Life's fleeting variations.

We hope this day will prove to be
   A time of happy pleasure,
A memory which both of you
   For many years will treasure!
           M.E.M.

For the New Baby!
Poems for Baby Congratulation Cards.

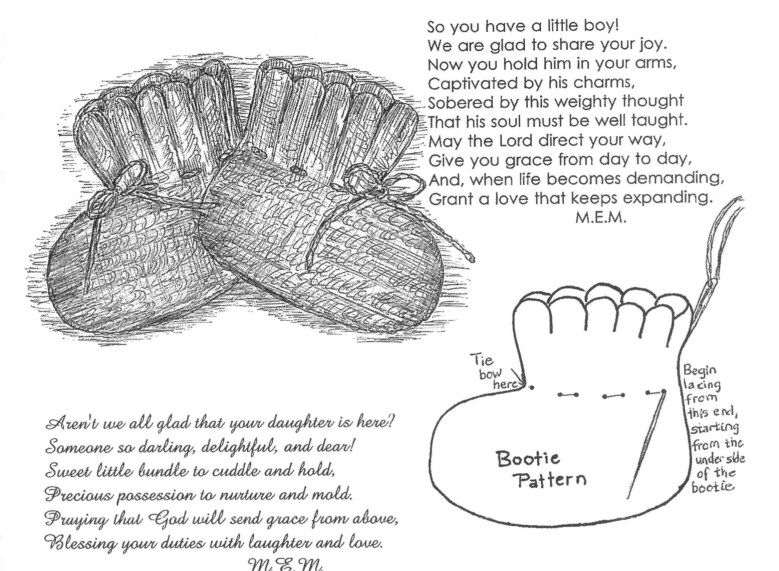

So you have a little boy!
We are glad to share your joy.
Now you hold him in your arms,
Captivated by his charms,
Sobered by this weighty thought
That his soul must be well taught.
May the Lord direct your way,
Give you grace from day to day,
And, when life becomes demanding,
Grant a love that keeps expanding.
M.E.M.

Tie bow here

Begin lacing from this end, starting from the under side of the bootie

Bootie Pattern

Aren't we all glad that your daughter is here?
Someone so darling, delightful, and dear!
Sweet little bundle to cuddle and hold,
Precious possession to nurture and mold.
Praying that God will send grace from above,
Blessing your duties with laughter and love.
M.E.M.

How to Make a Card with Baby Booties:
Make pattern. Draw around the pattern onto heavy-weight white paper, such as card stock. Cut out 2 booties, turning the pattern over for the second one so that the booties face the opposite way from each other. Using a pencil crayon, color them pink for a girl or blue for a boy. Draw in the details and shade the booties by coloring them darker along the edges and and along the detail.

Thread a yarn needle with baby yarn that matches the color of the booties. Holding the pattern and bootie together, poke the holes with the needle to mark where the yarn should go. Remove pattern. Double the yarn where it is laced through the bootie, taping the loose ends to the under side. When you have finished lacing the bootie, cut the yarn, leaving about 6". Separate the two strings and tie a bow. Trim ends. Do the same threading process for the other bootie.

Glue to the front of the card with white, multi-purpose glue. You may want to glue down only the foot and yarn part of the bootie. The top will stand away from the card a little, giving it a somewhat 3-dimensional look.

With Love to Mother and Father

Poems for Mother's Day and Father's Day

Note: "Mother" and "Father" may be used interchangeably in some of the poems. "Daddy" can be used instead of "Father" or "Papa", etc. to personalize it for your parent.

The words we children have to say
Are nothing new, we must confess.
We wish for you a Mother's Day
That's filled with joy and happiness.
                    M.E.M.

How to Make a Card with a Bow:
Trace the picture of the basket or single rose (next page) onto the front of the greeting card and color it. (Do not trace the bow.) Take a piece of narrow ribbon 9 inches long. Make a bow and trim ends. Glue into place with white multi-purpose glue.
Variation: You may want to use a picture of a flower or basket of flowers from an old greeting card or flower catalog instead of tracing one.

You're the dearest kind of mother
    and the best we've ever known,
And we're very, very thankful
    to regard you as our own.
We thank you for your mother love
    and all the things you do.
We want to reassure you
    of the love we have for you.
We'll have to be good children
    all this next year, anyway--
It's precious little else you'll get
    this year for Mother's Day.
                    M.E.M.

168

The same old message,
Yet freshly new--
We love you, Mama,
We surely do!   M.E.M.

A Mother's Day Message

If we would travel all around
    And search each town and country through,
No other mother could be found
    Who'd suit us half so well as you.

We thank you for the loving care
    You've given us since we were small,
The hours of toil, the words of pray'r,
    We thank you, Mama, for them all.

Why do we love you? You're our own
    Dear mother. Yes, that's why, it's true.
But it's not for this cause alone,
    It's also just because you're you!

No thrilling message write we here,
    Just what we've often said to you.
How glad we are that year by year
    The same old dear, sweet words are true!

                    M.E.M.

To You, Mama

It is very hard to find
Mothers of a better kind
    Than you, Mama.
Other mothers there may be
Who have lived most lovingly,
But who's best for such as we?
    You are, Mama!

Of your kind, unselfish ways
We are gladly bringing praise
    To you, Mama.
Who so freely lends a hand,
Giving up what she had planned,
Always tries to understand--
    Who but Mama?

We are wishing on this day
Happiness in ev'ry way
    To you, Mama.
Gentle love and sweet goodwill
You endeavor to instill
In our hearts which always will
    Love you, Mama!

                    M.E.M.

You're a very special person
　　And that we know right well,
And on occasions such as this
　　We're very glad to tell
You once again how very dear
　　You are the whole year through.
Of all the fathers in the world
　　There isn't one like you!　M.E.M.

November has Thanksgiving Day,
　　When days are turning cold.
We thank the Lord for giving us
　　His blessings manifold.
But halfway through the calendar
　　In June is Father's Day,
When children to their fathers have
　　Some special things to say.
"We love you much!" "You're wonderful!"
　　And, "You're the very best!"
These quotes, dear Papa, fit you well.
　　We echo them with zest.
But this day is a special time
　　For all us children, too,
Thanksgiving Day in June because
　　Our Papa dear is you!　　M.E.M.

How can it be that so many attest

Of all of the fathers their own is the best?

I won't undeceive them. They may think as they do,

But the reason they think so--They haven't had you!　　M.E.M.

How to Make a Picture Puzzle Card:
Choose and cut out a calendar picture for the front of the card. With a pencil make lines 3/4" apart all the way across the picture. Then draw lines 1" apart from the top to the bottom of the picture. With a felt-tip black marker make the squares interlocking. Outline around the edge of the puzzle with the marker. You may leave the picture whole, or you may very carefully cut out a few of the pieces Write, "Happy Father's Day," where you removed the puzzle pieces. Paste the puzzle pieces at the edge of the picture.

We hope each day throughout the year
　　Our words and deeds express
How that we children think of you
　　With loving tenderness.
But on this special Father's Day
　　A special word is due--
A hearty thanks for loving us
　　And, Papa, we love you!
　　　　　　　M.E.M.

With Heartfelt Sympathy *Poems for Sympathy Cards*

Revelation 21:4

And God shall wipe away all tears from their eyes and there shall be no more death, neither sorrow, nor crying, neither shall there be any more pain; for the former things are passed away.

Though the weight of the sorrow
    you're feeling just now,
  Must be painfully heavy to bear,
May it be of some comfort
    to know that your friends
  Remember you often in prayer.
             M.E.M.

Our hearts are saddened
    Because of your loss.
We're tempted to wish
    To remove this great cross.
How glad it would seem
    To make "all things right,"
And you could again
    Have hearts that are light.

But how dare we think
    For one moment we can
Improve on the All-Knowing
    Master's wise plan?
We bow our heads humbly
    Though sad be the way,
We trust He will help you
    For His comfort we pray.
May God give you patience,
    Though hard be the climb,
And strength to continue
    One day at a time.
             E.R.M.

May God be very near you
    As you journey on the way.
Though you miss your mother sadly,
    God will help you day by day.
May the blessed hope be near you
    That ALL is joy and love
Where one day you'll be together
    In that lovely HOME above.
             E.R.M.

How to Make a Card with a Scroll:
Trace the scroll onto a white paper. Write a comforting scripture verse on it. Cut out the scroll and paste it onto a piece of dark blue construction paper. Cut around the scroll, leaving about 1/8" of construction paper border.
Draw lines diagonally on the front of the card, using a dark blue pencil crayon. Glue the scroll into place on the front of the card. Place a flower sticker in front of the scroll.

I am the resurrection, and the life: he that believeth in me, though he were dead, yet shall he live: And whosoever liveth and believeth in me shall never die.

John 11:25+26

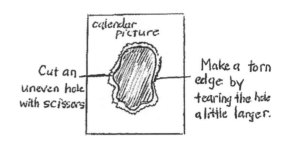

calendar picture

Cut an uneven hole with scissors

Make a torn edge by tearing the hole a little larger.

Although it hasn't been so long
Since we have known you well,
It seems you are our long-time friends.
And this we'd like to tell
That in our times together
We've grown to love and care,
And now our hearts are saddened
With the grief that you must bear,
And though your hearts are aching
May this knowledge help to heal
That our prayers are often with you
And we share the grief you feel.
E.R.M.

We do not know how God will give you comfort,
Nor in what way His peace will be distilled,
Nor what sweet voice shall whisper of His presence
Nor at what hour all this shall be fulfilled.
But this we know, God cares for all His children,
And to His word He always will be true,
And we are praying that His hand of mercy
Will touch your heart and softly comfort you.
M.E.M.

Only God's strength is sufficient to bear
The staggering weight of your cross.
Only the comfort that God can bestow
Can soften the pain of your loss.
Only God knows how deep and how dark
The valley you're now passing through.
But God is enough! His promise is sure,
"My grace is sufficient for you!"
M.E.M.

How to Make a Torn Frame for a Card:

Note: If you are making a sympathy card, remember to choose subdued colors and tranquil pictures.

Cut out a calendar picture a little smaller than the front of the card. Cut an uneven hole in the center. Slowly and carefully tear the hole a little larger to make the torn edges. It helps to hold both thumbs and fingers close together as you tear the edge with one hand and hold onto the frame with the other.

Paste the picture onto a piece of construction paper. Trim the construction paper around the outside of the picture, leaving about 1/8".

Cut out the center of the construction paper, leaving an inside border of about 1/2". Then carefully tear the construction paper, leaving about 1/4" exposed.

Paste onto the front of the card. Write a comforting scripture verse inside the frame.

Chapter Eight

FRIENDS AND RELATIVES

Table set for Thanksgiving guests
Centerpiece from a friend

Friends and Relatives

It is a compliment to the artificial flower when it is said to look "real." And it is a compliment to the real flower to be so healthy it looks artificial. In some ways, that is how it is with friends and relatives. It is a compliment to friends to be counted as family, and it is a blessing when relatives are also our friends.

This is a collection of poems written for or about our friends and relatives. Our friends have been *so very* good to us, and we have so many dear relatives, this short chapter seems quite inadequate. (Indeed Mary has written many more poems to our friends and relatives, but most of them are personalized.)

We are grateful to friends and relatives for all they mean to us and for all they have done for us. We feel blessed.

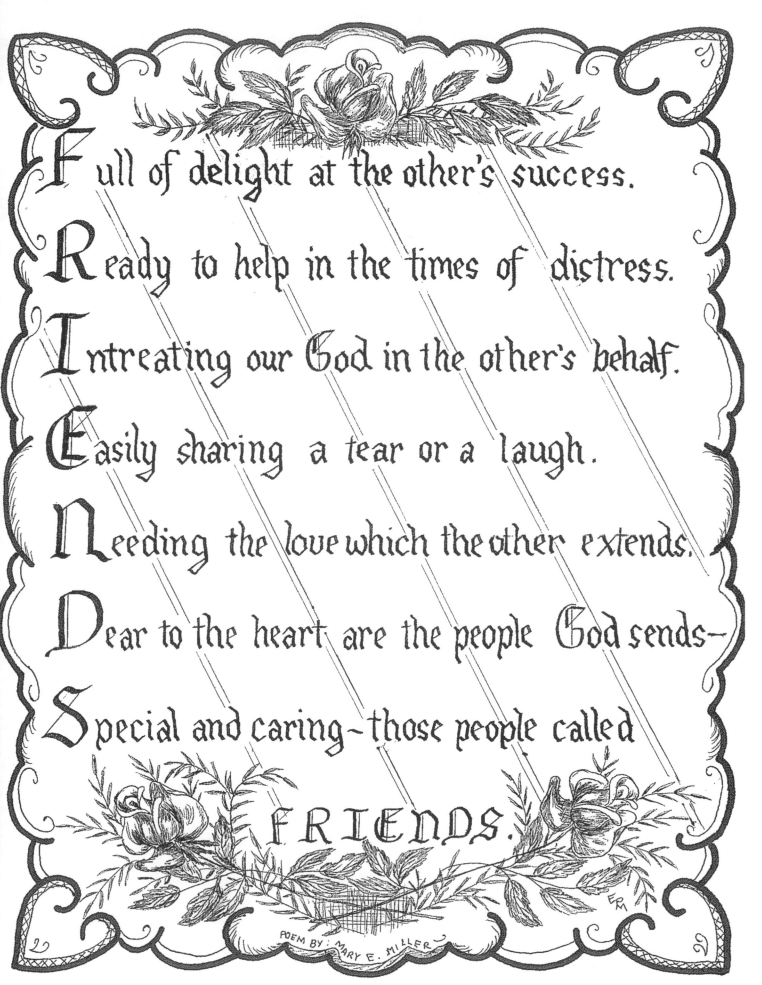

Full of delight at the other's success.

Ready to help in the times of distress.

Intreating our God in the other's behalf.

Easily sharing a tear or a laugh.

Needing the love which the other extends.

Dear to the heart are the people God sends—

Special and caring—those people called

FRIENDS.

POEM BY: MARY E. MILLER

To Our Neighbor

We used to often meet him as he peddled down the street.
He'd wave at us and we at him whene'er we chanced to meet.
We haven't seen him for a while because he has been ill.
And all of us are hoping that it won't be long until
He's well enough and strong enough to bike to town, for then
We'll know that things are back to rights and all is well again!

M.E.M.

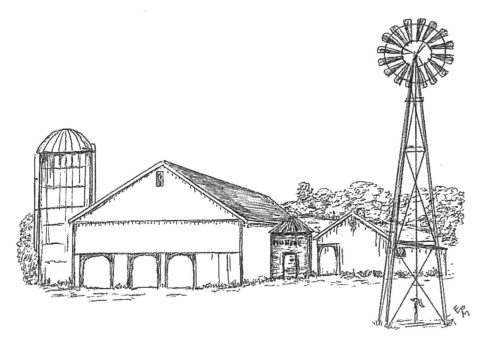

The Farmer

The farmer has chores he must do ev'ry day.
    Day laborers take a vacation.
The farmer at heart delights in his work
    And calls it a good occupation.
The labor is honest. The soil is his friend,
    And nature and he work together.
He patiently deals with weeds, pests, and disease.
    He keeps a sharp eye on the weather.
In springtime he plants his plowed fields with new hope.
    In summer he watches them growing.
In autumn he reaps them. In winter they rest.
    The seasons keep coming and going.
He thinks it no hardship to care for his stock,
    He finds them both friendly and charming.
He sleeps the good sleep of a laboring man.
    Yes, what could be better than farming?

Mary E. Miller

The Happy Man

To a smiling gentleman in a retirement center.

The man in the hall, as we pass him by
   A smile his face o'er spreads.
It makes me think of the warmth and light
   The summer sunshine sheds.

He can hardly walk and can scarcely speak,
   Yet many a conversation
Has given me less than his beaming smile
   In the way of inspiration.

So I lift up my chin and brush aside
   The thought of a petty trial.
It shames me to think of my gloominess
   When he lights up his smile.

Sometimes he may wonder what he can do
   In the way of things worthwhile.
I know what it is, for I'm often inspired
   By his generous, radiant smile.

I say to the man who sits in the hall,
   Keep smiling your smile so dear.
I'll try to pass on to those I meet
   Your happy smile of cheer.

           --E. Ruth and Mary E. Miller

A good name is rather to be chosen than great riches, and loving favour rather than silver and gold.
Proverbs 22:1

We Need Folks Like You

--Mary E. Miller

We need the lives of great, wise men
    To guide us like a star,
To show us what true purposes
    And aspirations are.
But how we need the common folks
    Who, in their humble way,
Show how to live a life for God
    In humdrum ev'ry day.

We need the gifted writer's lines.
    We need the poet's song.
But how we need the friendly word
    To cheer our souls along!
We need the good example
    Of honest lives and true.
We need the love and cheering smiles
    That come from folks like you!

Memory's Golden Threads

--Mary Elaine Miller

Sitting and rocking in silence,
　Eyes dreamy with thoughts long ago,
Hands folded in unwonted stillness,
　Tears dropping unheeded and slow,
A mother is weaving the mem'ries
　She wishes to treasure and keep
Of the son who lies on the hillside
　Enfolded in death's solemn sleep.

So strong was the tie that had bound them
　They could not be sundered apart
Without most painfully rending
　The strings of the fond mother-heart.
That pain is her constant companion
　And often the sigh and the tear.
Though she trusts he is happy in heaven,
　How sadly she misses him here.

So sitting there now in the stillness,
　Reviewing each memory's thread,
She is weaving a beautiful keepsake
　With the smiles and the looks of her dead.
Oh, precious the threads of her mem'ry!
　How welcome the blessed relief!
Preparing the heart for its healing
　By cleansing the wound made by grief.

She remembers his looks as a baby,
　Blue eyes and a little light hair,
The first words his baby lips uttered,
　How his first steps were taken and where.
A difficult child or a charmer,
　Depending which mood was his choice,
But the bad moods had slowly been conquered
　In a way that had made her rejoice.

Friends and neighbors have shared in her sorrow
　In the days since the death of her boy.
And some of the things they have told her
　She recalls with a bittersweet joy
And surprise, though of course she had noticed
　That he was exceptionally kind
And loving; but mothers see trifles
　To which other eyes may be blind.

But others had noticed. How precious
　The mem'ries they fondly had shared!
Of his bright, winning smile and his habit
　Of letting them know that he cared,
Of the help that he gave and his talent
　For putting a stranger at ease.
Could any declare the life useless
　Which had left such examples as these?

The spirit of love and compassion
　Expressed in the life of her son
Like a glad song of sweet inspiration
　Had been silenced when scarcely begun.
Perhaps those who listened with pleasure,
　Little thinking they ought to join in,
Have resolved in the silence of sorrow
　A song of their own to begin.

May that song never fail nor diminish
　But in beauty and volume increase,
Instilling in hearts sad and dreary
　A message of comfort and peace.
Blessed thought to the grief-stricken mother!
　What sweet consolation it brings!
Thus adding its own bit of beauty
　To the pattern of memory's strings.

So pondering long in the stillness,
　She quietly sits in her chair,
Weaving a tapestry golden,
　Weaving a tapestry fair.
And only those who have sorrowed
　After laying a child 'neath the sod,
Have known how blessed a healing
　Can be wrought by those mem'ries and God.

180

God's Servant

Brimming with vigor,
  Cheerful, enthused.
Happy wherever
  His help can be used.
Student of scripture,
  Eager to find
Roots, words, and meanings.
  Active in mind.
Bringing the message
  With earnest appeal,
Teaching, exhorting
  With whole-hearted zeal.
Faithful at bedsides,
  Offering pray'r,
Ever expressive
  Of kindliest care.
Present in sorrow
  In comforting ways.
Quick to encourage
  To strengthen and praise.
Blest is the pathway
  His eager feet trod.
Servant of mankind.
  Servant of God.

--Mary E. Miller

I Corinthians X

13. There hath no temptation taken you but such as is common to man: but God is faithful, who will not suffer you to be tempted above that ye are able; but will with the temptation also make a way to escape, that ye may be able to bear it.

To Encourage You

Haven't heard for quite a while just how you're doing.
Hope your good and worthwhile goal you're still pursuing.
    Though bad habits shrink from dying,
    Let it not prevent your trying.
May each morning give your strength a fresh renewing.

We are sending you this note just to remind you
Though discouragement and fear may search and find you
    And their presence is dismaying,
    We will keep on daily praying
That your struggle soon will be far, far behind you.

                                        M.E.M.

To a friend who asked us to pray for him when he wanted to quit smoking.

Excerpts from our Diary and Christmas Letters

Christmas letter, 1991: Uncle Joe and Aunt Lottie, from Oregon, were here a couple weeks this summer. Aunt Lottie helped us quilt the only quilt that we did this year. (Actually she did most of it-bless her heart!) It is a Grandmother's Fan. A neighbor gave us the quilt top.

April 11, 1992--Saturday: This was the day for the Marks reunion. All of the raisin-filled cookies we took were eaten. When Rachel and Stan left last week, we sent 2 cookies along for each of their family. We found out today that their dad tried unsuccessfully to buy Rachel and Stan's cookies. He was up to $2.50 per cookie.

May 23, 1996--Thursday: Around 11:15 our cousin and his wife, Edward and Sadie, and all their family stopped in. There were 55 of them traveling together in a bus. They didn't want to stay long, but Mary didn't realize that at first. She was in the house trying to figure out how to feed everyone!

April 19, 1999--Monday: Uncle Don and Aunt Madge, who recently moved to Constantine, MI, were here for dinner. Becky gathered dandelion for a salad, and Ruthie and Mama made steamed suet pudding with "Slidget," the Marks' name for the sauce. These are things Grandma Marks used to fix.

July 9, 1999--Friday: Mama, Becky, and Mary helped Uncle Don's family make cookies today. They made raisin-filled cookies and two other kinds--over 100 dozen in all.

May 30, 2000--Tuesday: Uncle Wilbert and Aunt Elva (Papa's sister) arrived for a visit last Wednesday. Last evening we invited 12 guests, friends from Aunt Elva's growing-up years. This afternoon Uncle Ben and Aunt Ruth (Papa's sister) arrived. For supper we invited eight other guests, cousins to Papa, Aunt Elva, and Aunt Ruth. We had a total of 22 entries in our guest book while Uncle Wilberts were here.

June 7, 2003--Saturday: The Miller reunion started at 8 o'clock this morning at Buffalo, Missouri, with registration and doughnuts. Around 850 people registered. (The family numbers 1449.) Kathy helped write the name tags and never did eat a doughnut! Aunt Ruth and Uncle Ben's family put a lot of work into making this reunion possible. Vernon, oldest of their 15 children, went ahead with the plans, making announcements and keeping things moving smoothly. The reunion was held at their school hall which was very adequate and comfortable. The kitchen is large and well-equipped, including large coolers, and generous folks from their church cooked and served the meals. All 850 of us were served in an amazingly short time. The family came from 20 states and from Costa Rica. We had devotions and then brunch. Around noon the families took turns standing up together. Then the first cousins stood together. There are about 80 of us and 53 were there. Papa's three sisters, Elva (Oregon), Mary (South Carolina), and Ruth (Missouri), were all there; but his brothers, Stanley (Mississippi), Joe and Harvey (Arizona) were unable to come. Lena, Alta, Alton, and David are no longer living. Before supper the aunts and uncles and older cousins shared memories of Daudy and Grandma. When the sun set in the evening, the sky was illuminated in brilliant colors, contrasted by the clouds. For devotions we sang, "Beyond the Sunset."

July 16, 2006--Sunday: About 24 Amish young folks ate a picnic here this afternoon. Afterward we joined them in singing hymns. We sat close to the dam, and with the high water, we had a lot of background music. This evening we went on a drive to the Union, MI, area where Mama was raised. Mama pointed out many places of interest including a hill where she went sledding once with a friend. The fun ended when Mama landed in the ditch. The next week she had a bad cold.

July 29, 2006--Saturday: What an eventful day! We picked 1 1/2 bushels of sweet corn last evening and 4 more bushels today. Our friends from Darien, IL, are spending the weekend in this area. Laura, age 14, helped pick and husk the corn. Arlene helped cut it off the cob, and Olivia, age 7, helped to put it into freezer boxes. We froze 24 quarts. Dinner, which we ate under the shade of the scarlet maple in our backyard, included corn on the cob, green beans, tomatoes, and a blueberry dessert. Samuel, 8 months, chewed on an ear, too. Daniel, age 3, says that Clara is really his dog but we just keep her. David and Sam worked on the waterwheel. They installed new connecting rods and have it working.

September 20, 2006--Wednesday: Papa's cousin Ralph and Lois, Greenwood, DE, spent most of the day with us. They helped us label applebutter, dig the gladiolus bulbs, mow yard, and pick 100 squash off our three hills of squash. We try to persuade them to move here.

February 7, 2008--Thursday: A 70-pound package containing 68 lemons arrived from a friend in Arizona. Some of them are huge. Last week Papa's cousin, Ira, sent a box of citrus fruit from their son's trees in Florida. Some of the fruit is a cross between a grapefruit and orange. They are delicious.

February 29, 2008--Friday: We have only 4 of the 68 lemons left. We have made lemonade, cookies, cake, mousse, lemon delight, and 43 pies. We have enjoyed sharing the lemon goodies with our friends. Those fresh lemons have an extra good flavor.

An aunt by kinship's claim.
Unique her role and part.
Nor is she only aunt by name,
True aunts are aunts in heart.

PERSPECTIVE

(A poem about Mama and Uncle Glenn.)

They were flashlight batteries,
   Used until they shone no more,
But to him who lined them up
   On the worn congoleum floor,

They were steeds of dashing strength,
   Swift of foot and bright of eye--
Much more thrilling than the dolls
   Which his sister held near by.

Sisters are so fun to tease!
   Turning to the mite he said,
"Look at all your darling dolls!
   Don't you know they're really dead?"

She was prone to sudden tears.
   She most likely cried right then.
But she had the spunk to say,
   "What about your horses, Glenn?"

Though we chuckle at this tale,
   Don't we often do that, too--
Look at our beloved things
   From a biased point of view?

Bright ideas of our own
   Look so splendid to our eyes,
But another's foolish dreams
   Are so easy to despise.

Tread with kind and tactful care.
   Let your words be choice and few.
How much different it looks
   From another's point of view!

--Mary E. Miller

A Generous Offer
(To Smile About)

Our cousin and his wife had one son and five daughters. When our cousin called to tell us the exciting news of the arrival of another son, we sent the following poem to his daughters.

Congratulations on that boy!
We're sure you're full of wild joy.
But listen, sisters, to this thought,
This brother that to you has brought
Such rapture will not always be
A darling bundle as you see
Today complete with charming smile
And pleasant cooing all the while.
For he'll grow up! It won't be bad
When he's done growing. What is sad
That while he's at it you will be
At odds with any such as he.
He'll pull your hair to make you cry
And hound you like the F. B. I.

He'll track in mud on fresh-washed floors.
He'll smear the windows, slam the doors,
Play in the dirt and dirty clothes.
He'll spray you with the garden hose.
He'll play some trick to make you squeal.
He'll pester you until you feel
Like shoving him right out the door
And hope to see him nevermore.
Before there is this dreadful fuss
Just give him, sisters, now to us.
Just think what anguish you will save
Yourselves. Come on now, girls, be brave!
He's sweet and cuddly now, but he
Won't stay that way, and so you see
You'd better give him now and quick
Before he makes you downright sick!

-- E. Ruth and Mary E. Miller

Jim Pressler's Story

Jim Pressler had a funny tale
    I wish to share with you.
He went to see a long-time friend.
    (This much of it was true.)
He found the friend out in the yard
    With mower cutting grass.
But in due time as mowers do
    It thirsted for more gas.
And as he filled the greedy thing
    A friendly cat strolled by,
He poured some gas upon its tail.
    (Such tricks I wouldn't try!)
The poor cat tore around the house--
    Yes, several times around.
At last it finally returned
    And sank upon the ground.

And here Jim paused to catch his breath
    As storytellers do.
Of course, we wondered what became
    Of that poor cat, don't you?
"Then did it die?" our mother asked,
    Thus kind of prompting him.
"Why, no, it just ran out of gas."
    Returned a smiling Jim.
I know not whence that story came--
    From hearsay or a book.
But how we laughed along with Jim
    To see how we'd "been took"!

Mary E. Miller

How good it is to think of friends!
And it is even better
To let them know of caring thoughts
By writing them a letter.

M.E.M.

Something amusing to call forth a smile,
Something uplifting and something worthwhile,
Something of life as it comes day by day
Small, common trifles of work or of play,
Bright optimism that looks for the better,
Put these in writing and send out a letter.

M.E.M.

The Mail

From runners on foot
    To wagons and trains,
From sailboats to steamships,
    From ponies to planes --

Across arid desserts,
    Or forests of trees,
Or flat, windswept grasslands,
    Or lands by the seas--

Who cares what conveyed it,
    Or what lands it went through?
We're glad we received it--
    A letter from you!

--Mary E. Miller

191

TELEPHONE OR LETTER?

Regarding the question,
   Which option is better,
Making a phone call
   Or writing a letter?--
If matters are urgent,
   The phone is the choice,
And then there's the pleasure
   Of hearing the voice.
However, the talking
   That's done on the phone
Is kept and preserved
   By the mem'ry alone.
But the data and pleasure
   A letter confers
Are all there in writing
   Through long after years.
          M.E.M.

So thanks a lot for writing!
   Life always seems to be
A little more exciting
   When a letter comes for me!
To read it is a pleasure,
   And it means so very much
To know your thoughts are with me
   And you want to keep in touch.
          M.E.M.

Chapter Nine

LESSONS IN THE SCHOOLHOUSE

A bulletin board display

School

A teacher's job is to help children learn, but the teacher often learns more than the students. I had heard or read this little observation before, but I certainly learned the truth of it when I was a teacher in a church school for three terms, (1999-2002). One of the most pleasant lessons was learning to know the people. I have been thankful many times for the friendships formed during this time.

This chapter contains several ideas for bulletin board displays. I was so busy when I was teaching that I was happy to have my sisters look after most of them. Later, though, when Becky and I made the displays for a former co-teacher, I found thinking of new ideas an interesting challenge. We picked up a few hints along the way which I hope others will find helpful.

1. Use Your Imagination. Change the ideas in this chapter to suit yourself.

2. Backgrounds. While paper is the best choice for the background of some displays, fabric works surprisingly well, and it can be reused many times. A background of cheerful print will do much to liven a somewhat drab display, but a quiet-toned background is good for a crowded, colorful one. Plastic party tablecloths will do though they are not as durable as the fabric.

3. Borders. It is nice if the border goes with the theme. Some of our favorites were waxed leaves (refer to the index to find "How to Wax Leaves") and snowflakes (directions included in this chapter under "How to Make Paper Snowflakes"). Often, though, we resorted to picking some ready-made borders out of the supply box. Sometimes we used paper from applebutter label backing for a plain white border.

4. Lettering. Letters cut from construction paper are ideal for legibility but time-consuming to make. We often used the 1 and 1/2 inch stencils for the poems. It saves a lot of time when mounting the display if the letters for each Bible verse or stanza of poem are glued onto a piece of paper, rather than stapling up each individual letter.

For smaller papers with shorter messages written with felt-tip marker, I would often place a paper with heavy black lines behind the paper on which I was writing. It helped me print more neatly without having to draw and erase lines every time.

5. Actual Items. Using a few actual items adds something to the display. (Examples: For "Preparation" the measuring spoons, measuring tape, embroidery project, seed packets, stalks of wheat, etc., can be "real" ones.) Straight pins are a real help in fastening these things to the board. Sometimes when we had a small item to display that couldn't be pinned, we cut a little "shelf" out of a small cardboard box. The shelf can be covered with pretty paper or fabric and pinned to the board.

6. Construction Paper Pictures. While these take some effort, they do add a nice effect. After we found the pictures we wanted, we often enlarged them on the copy machine. We used carbon paper to transfer them to the construction paper. Outlining the pictures with black or colored markers added a finishing touch.

7. Student Help. Several times when I was teaching, we had the students help us. We assigned different parts of the display to various groups of students. This was a great time-saver and lots of fun--in retrospect! I wouldn't have wanted to try it without help from my faithful sister!

8. Laying Out the Display. We did practically all the preparation of the displays at home. Before we made the 22-mile trip to the schoolhouse, we would measure off the size of the bulletin board on a flat surface and lay out the display. Then we could decide if we had enough items and how to arrange them.

9. Putting Up the Display. Use straight sewing pins to tack items to the board until you have all of them properly arranged, then staple them down. This helpful tip from a former teacher saved us a lot of time.

10. Disposing of Used Displays. If you do not wish to keep them, perhaps you would know of some other teacher who would be happy for them.

And now a word about the souvenir on the last page of this chapter. I certainly do not know all the history of school souvenirs, but they must have been somewhat common in the early 1900's. We have some from that era from both sides of our family.

Keep your eyes and heart open to the rewards of teaching, and appreciate them to the full!

--Mary E. Miller

S teady, dependable, diligent, neat,

C arefully working till goals are complete,

H elpful and cheerful and willing to share,

O pen and honest and friendly and fair,

O thers promoting, respecting each rule,

L et this be said of each one in our school.

M.E.M.

A NEW BEGINNING

Our workbooks and this term of school
   Are fresh and clean and new,
But, sadly, we will make mistakes
   Before the year is through.

But learning is our aim and goal,
   Not pages blank and white.
We'll strive to keep our errors few,
   And those we make, make right.
          M.E.M.

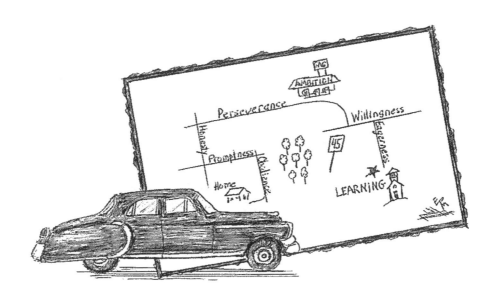

Be Prepared

Are you ready for the journey
    Through the coming term of school?
Is your tank filled to the brimming
    With Ambition as the fuel?

Is your youthful brain, the engine,
    All in tune to do its best?
Does your battery have power
    To begin each day with zest?

Make your destination Learning.
    To directions give good heed.
And remember careful working
    Gains more ground than reckless speed.

M.E.M.

School Lunch Blessing - MEM & ERM

We bow our heads in gratitude
And ask Thy blessing on this food.
We thank Thee, Lord, for Thy great love
And all the blessings from above.
May Thou be with us through this day
And watch us while we work and play.
May our desire ever be
To love and serve and follow Thee.
In Jesus' Name,
Amen.

199

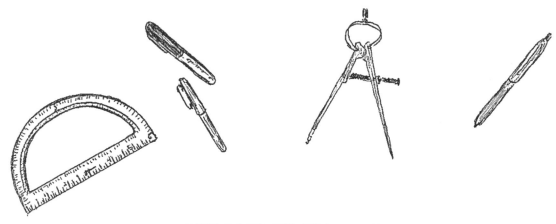

WHAT IT TAKES

You may have the best of talents,
    Books, and instruments for writing,
Best of education systems,
    Desks, resources, rooms, and lighting.

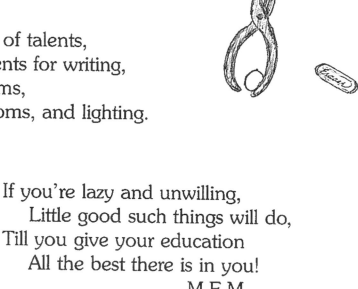

If you're lazy and unwilling,
    Little good such things will do,
Till you give your education
    All the best there is in you!
                        M.E.M.

Color

Red for roses.

Green for leaves.

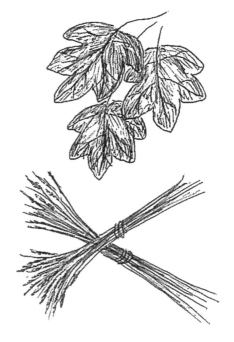

Black for midnight.

Gold for sheaves.

Gray for bleak skies.

Blue when clear.

White for snowflakes.

Brown for deer.

Some are vivid.

Some are duller.

All God's earth

Is full of color.

M.E.M.

Suggestion: Cut letters for each line out of construction paper, using the color mentioned in the line. The last two lines could be multi-colored.

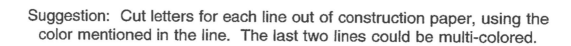

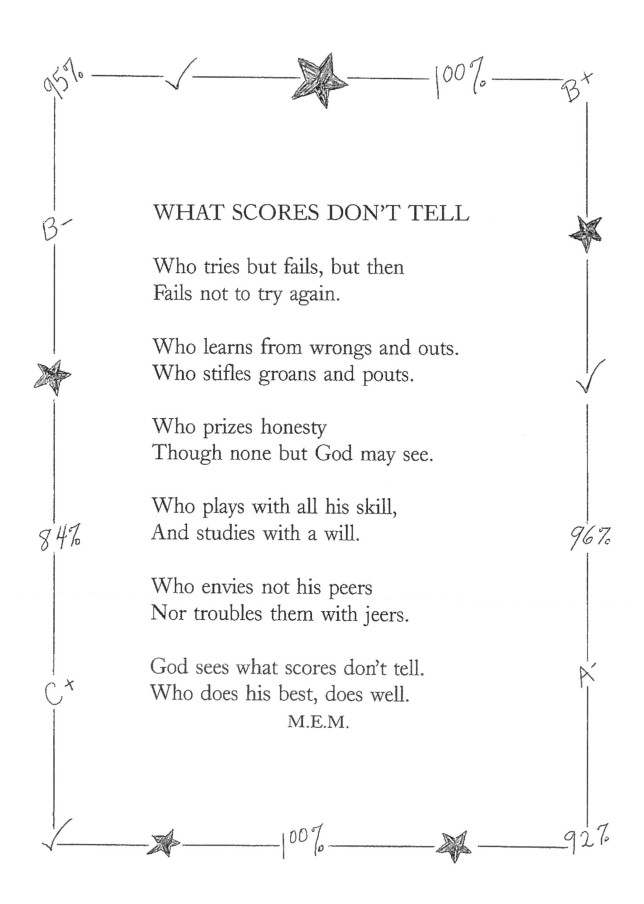

WHAT SCORES DON'T TELL

Who tries but fails, but then
Fails not to try again.

Who learns from wrongs and outs.
Who stifles groans and pouts.

Who prizes honesty
Though none but God may see.

Who plays with all his skill,
And studies with a will.

Who envies not his peers
Nor troubles them with jeers.

God sees what scores don't tell.
Who does his best, does well.

M.E.M.

What Scores Can't Tell

A score can name the winning team
    Or academic star,
But scores alone cannot tell who
    The winners really are.

Who gave his studies all his best?
    Who played with all his might?
Who worked with dogged patience till
    The answer came out right?

Who did not taunt the losing team?
    Who meekly took an out?
Who met detested work or play
    Without complaint or pout?

What scores can tell is, after all,
    The unimportant part.
The world looks on the outward man,
    But God looks on the heart.

--Mary E. Miller

Little by Little

Little by little,
    Bit by bit,
We'll get done
    If we keep at it.

Little by little,
    Piece by piece,
Never let
    Our labors cease.

Perseverance
    Is what we need,
Not a great
    Increase of speed.

Not so much
    A test of skill,
But endurance
    Of the will.

Little by little,
    One by one,
This is the way
    Great tasks are done.

                --Mary E. Miller

Spend or Save?

Only a penny wasted here,
    Only a nickel there.
Foolish extravagance is not cheap.
    The money is gone, but where?

Only a penny saved today,
    Only a nickel or dime.
Slowly the savings accumulate,
    A little bit at a time.

Little by little the habit grows.
    Money is saved or spent.
Happy is he who can do without.
    Woe to the discontent!
                    M.E.M.

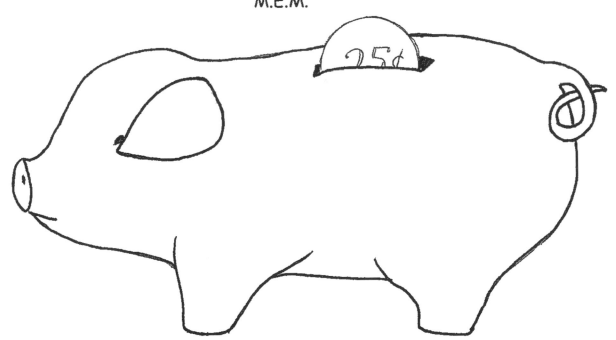

How to Make Aluminum Foil Coins:

"Coins" can be made for the piggy bank by using aluminum foil. Press a piece of aluminum foil over a coin and cut it out carefully with the coin still in place. Press it again before removing the coin.

Cut a small piece of clear tape. Fold and stick the tape over itself and put it under the aluminum foil coin. Place the coin on the poster. Since the aluminum foil easily looses the imprint, it must be handled *very* carefully. This will take a little practice and even so they will probably be imperfect.

Important Knowledge

The purpose of school is to fill ev'ry mind
With all the best knowledge a teacher can find.
Arithmetic, grammar, historical facts,
And laws scientific on which nature acts.

Such knowledge is practical, useful, and good.
But higher the knowledge that each teacher should
Endeavor to give to each eager young soul,
The knowledge which makes ev'ry day beautiful.

Of cheerfulness, kindness, and strict honesty,
The will to do labor industriously,
Compassion which reaches to others in need--
All those who learn these are blest students indeed!
                                        M.E.M.

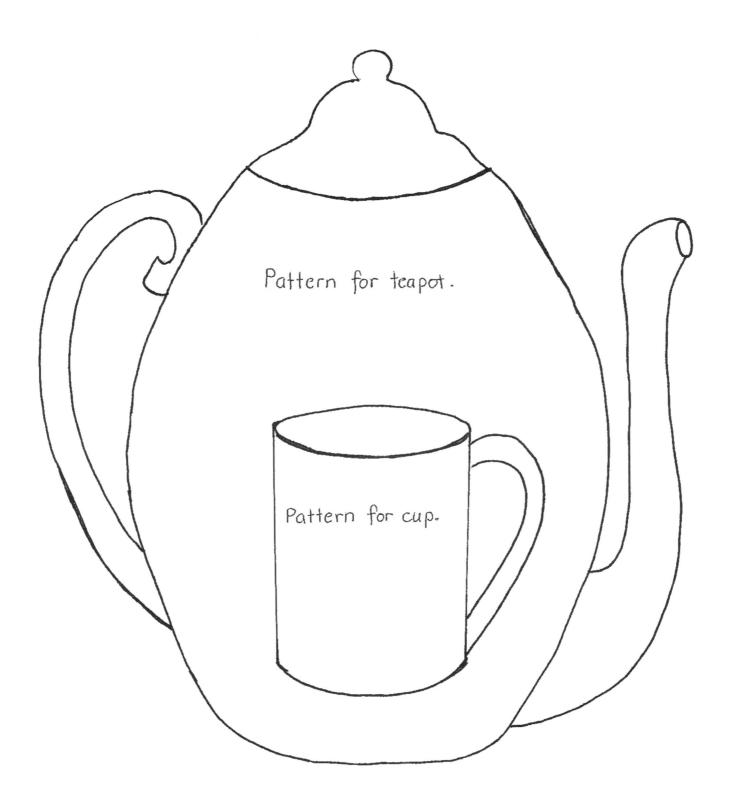

Pattern for teapot.

Pattern for cup.

Suggestion: Have the pupils draw their own designs on their cups.

Don't Just Sit and Dream

Don't sit upon the siding
    While the other trains go by.
Don't watch the people riding
    With a wistful, dreamy eye.
Ease out into the railway.
    Work up a bit of steam.
You really can go places
    If you don't just sit and dream.
            M.E.M.

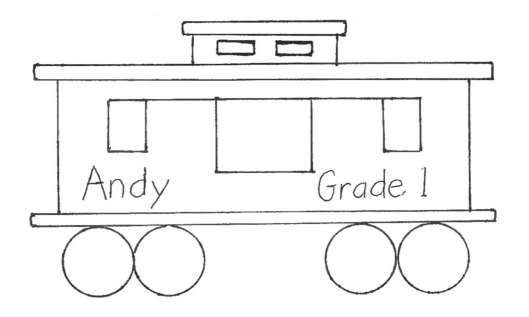

PAY ATTENTION!
DON'T LET YOUR TRAIN OF THOUGHTS DERAIL,
FOR THEN YOU'RE APT TO LOSE IT.
THE ABSENT-MINDED OFTEN FAIL.
JUST KEEP YOUR HEAD AND USE IT!
M.E.M.

Our teacher gave us patterns of a boxcar and a tank car. We chose one to make out of construction paper. We wrote our name and grade on the car. Then she lined the train up on a wall with her name on the engine.

Enlarge these patterns to the size you want.

THE POEM TRAIN

--Mary E. Miller

A poem with an empty thought
   Is like an empty train,
And though it travels as it ought
   Its travels are in vain.

A poem's usefulness depends
   Upon the load it bears.
The warmth its lifting thought extends,
   The humor which it shares.

Upon the Literary Road
   It travels near and far.
The title is the engine's code,
   Each verse another car.

It pulses grandly down the track
   With singing iron wheels.
The rhythm is the click and clack
   And throb the reader feels,

Until an awkward syllable
   Creates a stirring jar.
Then watch a bit of cargo roll
   And tumble from that car.

Imperfect rhyme disrupts the tone
   And sets the readers back,
And words employed for rhyme alone
   Can throw the train off track.

So choose your cargo carefully
   And give your train your best
So those who read your lines may be
   Instructed, helped, and blest.

A Poet

The life of a poet
    must be fun.
He'll sit under a shade tree,
    or in the sun;

Nothing to do
    but keep on writing.
Sometimes things are dull,
    but they're usually exciting.

I'd like to be a poet,
    but I cannot see
How the life of a poet
    could ever fit me.

--Alta I. Marks (Now Alta I. Miller.)
Constantine High School
Printed in a book of poems
written by area high school students.

The Daughter's Reply

I've found that so often my mother is right.
    She certainly was that time!
I wouldn't be happy if all of my hours
    Were fettered to rhythm and rhyme.
But though I am thankful to work with my hands,
    It gives me great joy now and then
To reach for the poem that runs through my head
    And seize it with paper and pen. --Mary E. Miller

Excerpts from our Diary and Christmas Letters

Christmas letter, 1999:   In September Mary began teaching the fourth, fifth, and sixth graders at a Christian school. It is a 35-minute drive from home. This summer a classroom was added to the school so she has a nice, new room.

Mary ("Miss Miller") has 19 eager, happy children in her room. It has been a challenge to get the assignments worked in, and there is a great deal of homework for Mary. We other girls help her when we can. Despite the added work load and full schedule, this teaching job has many rewards. It is good to hear the children's delighted laughter at lunchtime and recess, to hear them say, "I'll try!" when they have a difficult assignment, and to have their willing behavior with the knowledge of the parents' support.

December 10, 1999--Friday: Every Friday afternoon Mary's school has an hour of art class. Today we started crochet classes (Becky and Ruthie went to help). The children wanted to learn how to make granny squares. Most of the boys are not so happy to be included in this class--crocheting is for girls, you know! One of the mothers came to help, and a father kindly came along to show his interest in the project. This father learned how to knit when he went to school and can knit mittens and socks.

February 18, 2000--Friday: Becky knew two of Mary's fourth-graders would have some spare time today so she sent a note to them asking them to check some workbooks. Becky had written in the note, "Thanks for your help," and that puzzled Jordan. He had not helped Becky yet so why was she thanking him? Mary explained to him that Becky was thanking him in advance. "Oh," he said, "That's getting the effect before the cause!" (They have been studying cause and effect in language.)

Christmas letter, 2000: One project this summer was inviting Mary's 19 pupils and their families for supper. We did it in seven evenings, and each time it was pleasant enough to eat outside at the three picnic tables. Each time we served basically the same menu so by the end of the summer we had it about down to a science!

Christmas letter, 2002: Since Mary decided not to teach this fall, she was given a comforter with the names of all her pupils.

January 27, 2006--Friday: The last three Friday afternoons Mary, Becky, and/or Ruthie have been helping with a crocheting class at the school where Mary used to teach. Today the children starting making granny squares. One boy wanted to make "grandpa squares" instead.

Poems written by
Mary Miller's
Fourth Grade Class
for a Language Arts assignment

The Lord Is Good
by Louis

The Lord is good! The Lord is good!
The Lord is good to me.
And when life's way is over,
I will dwell in eternity.

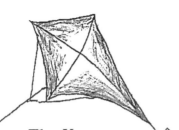

The Kite
by Jordan

One day I saw a bright red kite
Gently blowing in the breeze.
It looked so beautiful in flight--
So beautiful and free.

My New Baby Brother
by Leah

He's so chubby and sweet.
I hold him each day.
And, "Will you come see him?"
Is what we will say.

"Clang, Clang, Bang, Bang"
by Rhoda

"Clang, clang, bang, bang,"
Goes the fire truck.
If the water shoots at me,
I should always duck!

Kitten in a Basket
by Japheth

I can't find my kitten--
Oh! yes, in a little basket.
My little kitten is dead.
What shall I do for a casket?

Crocheting
by Courtney

I like to work with yarn;
It is so nice and warm, you see.
I like to make granny squares
To make an afghan just for me.

My Dolly
by Lydia

I have a little dolly.
Her name is Floppy Nellie.
She calls me, "Lovely Mom,"
And calls herself, "Sweet Ellie."

How To Make Paper Snowflakes

 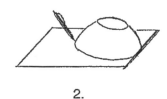 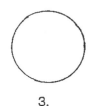

1.   2.   3.

1. Find a round object the size you want your snowflake.
2. Trace around the round object onto a white sheet of paper.
3. Cut the paper circle out.

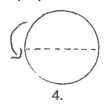 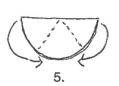

        4.   5.   6.

4. Fold the circle into half.   5. Fold the half into thirds.   6. Fold into half again.

7. Cut a variety of shapes from both sides, being careful to leave some of it intact. Cut off the point and cut a design in the top.

8. Unfold.

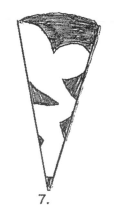 

       7.   8.

Keep practicing, using your own imagination. No two snowflakes are exactly alike. These are simple for children to make.

****

White snowflakes make a nice border for a bulletin board against a dark blue background. Sometimes our teachers would tape a piece of sewing thread to the snowflake and hang them from the ceiling.

S nowflakes, all six-sided, are

N onetheless unique.

O f divine creative pow'r

W ordlessly they speak.

F ragile individuals,

L oners melt away.

A ll together, though, they can

K eep the world at bay.

E v'rything in winter dress

S hows the snowflakes' loveliness.

M.E.M.

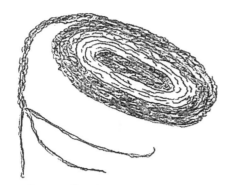

DRAW A BIRD

1. draw circle.

2. attach a smaller circle.

3. add a tail.

4. add detail. erase unwanted lines.

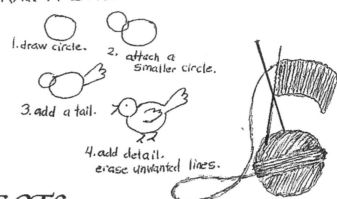

WINTER PROJECTS

When winter makes you stay inside,
It's pleasant to be occupied.
So choose a hobby of some kind,
And learn new skills of hand and mind.

STAMP COLLECTING
Can be an inexpensive and an educational hobby.

or---

When the mercury drops and the cold winds blow
And the fields and the slopes are covered with snow,
How pleasant to sit where it's cozy and snug,
Carving a chain or braiding a rug!
Away with complaining, "There's nothing to do!"
Hobbies make keepsakes and memories, too.

or--

When outdoor excitement you cannot pursue,
Plenty of projects are waiting for you.
                    M.E.M.

Note: Sometimes Mary writes more than one poem before she comes up with one that suits her. She decided to include the three versions of *Winter Projects* here and let you choose which one suits you the best.

TIME

Our time is a gift from God.
Consider each moment a prize.
Endeavor to use ev'ry day, ev'ry hour
In a way that is helpful and wise.
M.E.M.

In the beginning God created the heaven and the earth. Genesis 1:1

And the angel...sware by him that liveth for ever and ever...that there should be time no longer.
Revelations 10:5&6

And God said, Let there be lights in the firmament of the heaven to divide the day from the night; and let them be for signs, and for seasons, and for days, and years. Genesis 1:14

How to Make a Paper Plate Clock:

Have your young students make these clocks to teach them how to tell time. Call out a time such as "9:30," and see how quickly they can set their clocks.

Use a plain paper (not plastic) plate. Write the numbers on the plate using a heavy marker or a crayon.

Punch a hole in the center of the paper plate.

Make hands out of black construction paper or light weight cardboard. Punch holes near the bottom of the hands.

Put a brad through the holes in the hands and paper plate so that the hands can be moved.

• Pattern for hour hand.

• Pattern for minute hand.

WHAT'S IN A GALLON?

We are the cups.
 We are little and small.
There are sixteen of us
 And it takes us all
To fill up a gallon.
 The pints, you see,
Are exactly twice
 As big as we.
Because they are larger,
 It takes only eight
To fill up a gallon.
 (Did you get that straight?)
Now here is the quart,
 And what do you do
To fill it up?
 One pint times two.
Now this one is easy
 For many a scholar--
It takes four quarters
 To equal a dollar.
Remember that number.
 Forget it no more.
To fill up a gallon
 One quart times four.
Now here's half a gallon.
 The name gives a clue.
To make one whole gallon
 Of course, it takes two.

--Mary E. Miller

Suggestion: Use this poem for a poster and the following one for memorization.

A Lesson on Measures
We'll keep this thing short.

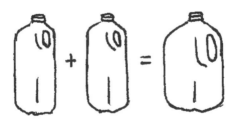

Two cups in a pint.

Two pints in a quart.

Two quarts--half a gallon.

Two halves make a whole.
So here is a gallon.
The gallon is full.
                    --Mary. E. Miller

Do Your Best

Don't trudge each day
On the dreary way
    Of SCARCELY-GOOD-ENOUGH.
For the lazy man
And the careless man
    Find going slow and rough.

But set your sights
For the splendid heights,
    And work with care and zest.
Train your attitude
For the altitude
    Of the sphere of DO-YOUR-BEST.
      M.E.M.

Pattern for kite.

How to Make Kites to Use as Incentives:
Have your students cut kites out of cardboard. Cover them with construction paper or color them. Have the students write their names and grades on them. Punch a hole near the bottom of the kite. Cut a yard of heavy string and fasten it in the hole. Cut at least two different colors of flags, using felt or any other suitable material. Cut the flags 1 1/2" x 4". As the children earn the flags, add them to the string. Fasten the flag by making a slip knot (running knot) in the string. Slip the flag into the loop. Pull the knot tightly around the center of the flag.
Example of incentive guide: Spelling test grades: Red flags=100%. White flags= 90%-99%.

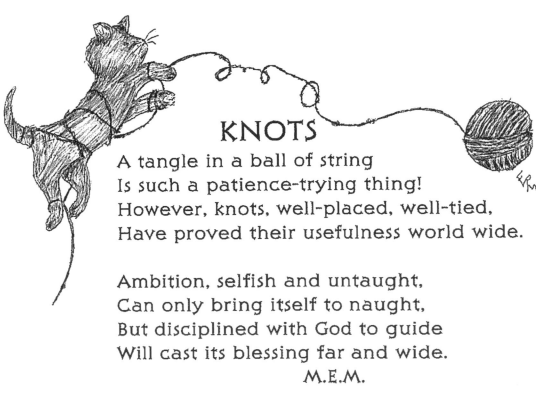

KNOTS

A tangle in a ball of string
Is such a patience-trying thing!
However, knots, well-placed, well-tied,
Have proved their usefulness world wide.

Ambition, selfish and untaught,
Can only bring itself to naught,
But disciplined with God to guide
Will cast its blessing far and wide.

M.E.M.

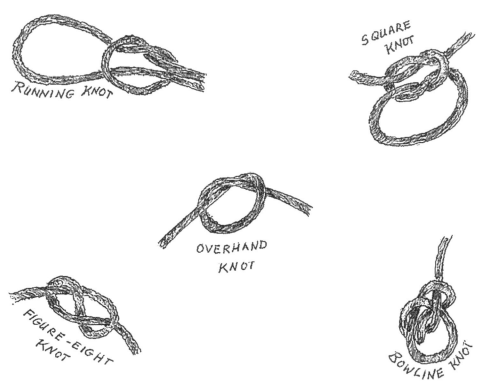

RUNNING KNOT

SQUARE KNOT

OVERHAND KNOT

FIGURE-EIGHT KNOT

BOWLINE KNOT

Suggestion: Use rope or braided twine to make actual knots. Look up *knot* in the dictionary or encylclopedia for more illustrations on various knots. You may also want to include illustrations of different ways knots are used. Examples: tatting, sailboat, hay bale, shoe, comforter, etc.

OF SPRING AND YOUTH

It isn't enough to rejoice in the spring,
In the promise and hope of each growing, new thing,
For we must not live for the springtime alone,
There are fields to be plowed. There are seeds to be sown.
Observe springtime beauties. Delight in them all,
But plant your seeds now for the harvest next fall.

Bright hopes for the future, health, laughter, and fun
Are blessings of youth so enjoy each one.
But just as the morning gives way to the noon,
The cares of adulthood will rest on you soon.
So give to today all your highest and best
That all of your future by God may be blest.
                    M.E.M.

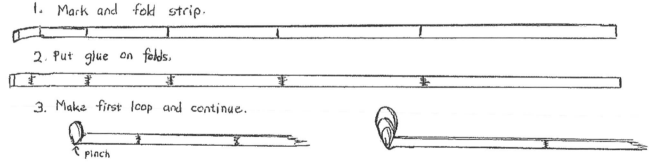

How to Make Flowers Using Paper Strips:
Using colored paper, cut strips about 5/8" wide. (We were able to procure some ready-cut strips at a print shop.) Glue strips together, overlapping ends about 1/2", to make a piece about 44 1/2" long.
1. Mark and fold strip at the following intervals: 1/2", 4", 9", 15 1/2", 23 1/2", 33", and 44".
2. Lay strip out flat. Starting at the end you marked first, skip first fold. Smear each of the remaining folds with a stick of glue, covering a spot about an inch long.
3. Holding the first fold, bring strip around to form a circle and pinch second fold firmly over first. Bring strip around over first circle and pinch third fold over second, repeat with rest of folds. For each flower make six of these with flower-colored paper and two of green paper for leaves. Take a piece of paper about the size of the flower and squeeze about an inch circle of multi-purpose glue in the middle. Lay the points of the petals on the glue. Put a large drop of glue where you want each leaf and lay points of leaves on the glue. Allow to dry.

SPRING CLEANING

It's time to clean the corners,
　　To throw the trash away,
To scrub and dust and vacuum,
　　Removing disarray.

Lord, help us clean the corners,
　　And take the trash away
From our young minds, and fill them
　　With good things ev'ry day.
　　　　　　R.I.M.

CREATE IN ME A CLEAN HEART, O GOD, AND RENEW A RIGHT SPIRIT WITHIN ME.

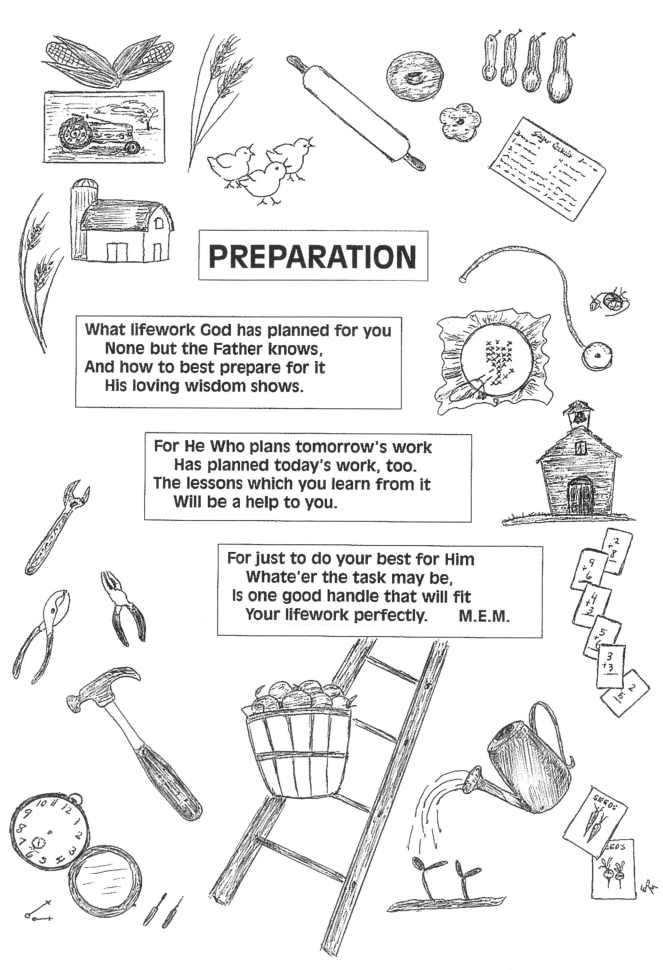

PREPARATION

What lifework God has planned for you
    None but the Father knows,
And how to best prepare for it
    His loving wisdom shows.

For He Who plans tomorrow's work
    Has planned today's work, too.
The lessons which you learn from it
    Will be a help to you.

For just to do your best for Him
    Whate'er the task may be,
Is one good handle that will fit
    Your lifework perfectly.   M.E.M.

224

School-Day Countdown

Vacation's coming! How the outdoors calls us
    With birds and flow'rs, green grass, and warming sun!
But there's still work to do inside the schoolroom;
    Let's tackle it until the job's well done.

Soon closed will be our books, also our schoolroom;
    At rest will be the pencil and the pen.
The girls will learn housekeeping from their mothers,
    And growing boys will work beside the men.

We also dream of times of summer leisure
    For playing, fishing, picnics, and the rest,
But let's dig in right now and try our hardest;
    Vacation's sweetest when we've done our best.

We ask the Lord that He will bless our lessons
    Both from the books and those in books not found,
And let's return to work with renewed vigor
    When summer's gone and autumn comes around.

                    --Rebecca I. Miller

SOUVENIR

Miss Mary Miller
Fourth and Fifth Grade Teacher

May 11, 2002

Pupils	
Fourth Grade	
Isaac	Melody
Evan	Sophia
Judith	Joseph
Alex	Timothy
Fifth Grade	
Orv	Janita
Clement	Matthias
Ross	Marletta

At Close of School~

Our pencils and our school books
 We gladly put away.
The ending of this happy term
 We celebrate today.

Although I knew you none too well
 Last fall when school was starting,
I find it tugs me at the heart
 To think upon our parting.

How many lessons, great and small,
 You children have been learning!
As needed, may you through the years
 Find every one returning.

God bless the mem'ries of this place!
 Those gems we hoard and treasure.
They'll give in long and lonely hours
 Diversion and great pleasure.

Let not the thought of past mistakes
 Continue to distress us,
But may the good we learned from them
 Return at length to bless us.

Of what your life may hold for you
 I have not one prediction.
May God go with you, Everyone!
 Shall be my benediction.

— Miss Miller

Note: Mary wrote the above poem for a school souvenir pamphlet. She gave one to each of her pupils on the last day of school.

Chapter Ten

SONGS FROM THE
SICK ROOM

Roses on the fence beside the old milk house

WHAT'S IN THE NEST?

I found a little grassy nest
  In our round flowerbed.
I was not happy at the sight,
  For I was filled with dread.

"I hate to think of it," I mused.
  "But I should kill those mice.
This job of killing animals
  I do not think is nice.

"I do believe it is a job
  More suited to the men."
But Papa and my brother Sam
  Were not close by right then.

I took a little garden spade,
  And, moving gingerly,
I lifted off the grassy top
  To see what I would see.

There, lying snugly in that hole,
  Were bunnies, soft and round.
I was delighted that it was
  Not mice that I had found.

Then Becky, who was standing by,
  Said, "There's a lesson here.
Not everything we dread turns out
  As badly as we fear."

So when I see the bunnies now
  I think of what she said,
And try to face the day with trust
  Instead of fear and dread.

                - Mary Elaine Miller

MY CHEER-UP BIRDS

On days when I'm tired and I feel a bit blue,
And the things I accomplish are very few,
When staying cheerful seems rather hard,
I've found two helpers in our own backyard.
There's a sleek, gray catbird and a perky wren,
And they pause at their labors now and again.
The little wren sings with a merry trill,
And the catbird warbles at his own sweet will.
It seems these two happy birds are bent
To fulfill the mission on which they are sent.
And their cheery songs bring to my lips a smile,
And my heart grows lighter all the while.
Oh, are we not grateful to God that He sends
Such notes of good cheer by our feathered friends?

                                        --Mary E. Miller

On the Sea of Ill Health

(To others who are also fighting cancer.)

Columbus sailed the unexplored
  And unfamiliar sea
With sailors, angry, restless men
  Who threatened mutiny.
He kept his face set forward, and
  He would not turn around.
At last he glimpsed a speck of light
  And knew that land was found.

And we, like brave Columbus, find
  Ourselves adrift at sea
With Dread, Self-pity, Fear, and Doubt
  And Gloom for company.
The Land of Health has banished us
  From off its sunny coast.
"And nevermore will they return,"
  The guarding watchers boast.
Our watchword ever must be, "On!"
  The face be forward set.
Who knows what blessings may await,
  What joys may crown us yet?
If Doubt and Dread and Bleak Despair
  Be prisoned by God's pow'r,
Then Faith and Peace and Comfort may
  Go with us ev'ry hour.

At last the eager eyes shall see
  A glowing speck of light,
And very soon the welcome land
  Shall break upon our sight.
Then some of us shall find ourselves
  In Land of Health Restored.
What thankfulness and gratitude
  Shall from the heart be poured!
Not one shall know how long his feet
  May tread that happy shore,
Nor if the time shall come for him
  To sail the sea once more.
But God can take away all Fear
  And give us Faith instead,
For those who love the will of God
  Have nothing more to dread.

For some the waiting land shall lie
  Beyond the Bar of Death,
Where weary eyes shall close in sleep,
  And quenched shall be the breath.
But those who truly loved the Lord
  And listened to His voice,
Shall find themselves where praise abounds
  And angel bands rejoice.
There none shall wonder just how long
  His happy stay shall be,
For all redeemed shall live with God
  And Christ eternally.

So, Fellow Captains, when the sea
  Is stormy, wild, and rough,
When you believe your weary heart
  Has suffered quite enough,
Remember God can be your strength
  When all your strength is gone,
And never turn your ship around
  But keep on sailing on!

                —Mary Miller

My Voyage on the Sea of Ill Health

What would my life have been like if I would not have had cancer? I do not know. The years since that memorable May of 2001, have not been easy. We have, however, learned many valuable lessons. Perhaps the most valuable of all is the reinforcement of the knowledge that God is real, He does care, and He is a God of love.

When the doctor told me on May 3, 2001, that I had colon cancer, it was not what we wanted to hear, but the picture the doctor painted of surgery and how it would affect me later sounded easily manageable. I had a pre-op CT scan on May 8.

May 10 found us in the doctor's office again. The doctor took my hand, and in his kind, fatherly way told me that the CT scan showed multiple nodules (which were almost certainly cancer) on both lobes of the liver. Surgery was not an option; chemotherapy was all he could suggest, but it would be good to have more testing done in the unlikely event that it was something benign.

We walked out of the office to the car. I was so naive I thought I'd likely have a number of years yet to live. Even so, I felt like the world had stopped. It seemed to take an effort just to walk, but I tried to hold myself together.

It was not easy to break the news to the rest of the family. A long night followed without much sleep and with many tears and prayers. We wrote down a number of comforting Bible verses which suddenly stood out with new meaning.

The next day Papa and I went to tell several of our neighbors about my CT scan. I called friends and relatives on the telephone. I couldn't think of anything else so it was a relief to talk about it. Everyone was very kind.

As the days wore on, it was very difficult to know how to go about further testing and what to do about treatment. I saw several doctors, and wouldn't you know it, they couldn't agree what to do. And in the meantime we could imagine the cancer growing rapidly. We were thankful I felt so well. I could imagine a pain in my right side, but I really wasn't sure if it was in my liver or in my head! And I looked the very picture of health.

After two oncologists looked at the scans and said they didn't feel it was conclusive that those spots were cancer, it did make us feel better. The blood tests came back well within normal limits, and our hopes rose a little more. Still, the doctors kept saying they couldn't tell for sure without further testing. The incident related in the poem, "What's in the Nest?" took place during this time.

May 30 is another memorable date. Papa, Mama, and I went to the doctor's office to learn the results of an MRI I had taken the week before. At very best I was hoping the scan would not show positively that there was cancer. We were called into the little room, and the nurse did the blood pressure and all the other routine checks and questions. She seemed very interested in my case and had the nerve to read the report--silently, of course--right in front of us! Although she tried to remain expressionless, somehow the look on her face made me feel a tiny bit more hopeful.

Then the doctor came in. (You can imagine how my heart was pounding!) He shook hands and asked how we were, but he did manage to get to the point surprisingly quickly. He scanned the report, humming his typical little tune, then looked up. He extended his hand to me with a smile and said, "Good news! There is no cancer on the liver!"

We called home before we left Goshen. Becky, who had been working in the lower garden, sat down on the grass before she answered the portable phone. She was so happy she sat there and cried. Our ride home was surprisingly quiet. I'm not sure I had realized before that at times one can be silenced by happiness. I had a lot of telephone calls to make, and how wonderful it was to have good news to share!

After that experience, a mere colon resection didn't seem like such a big thing. It was scary enough though when the time drew closer. The surgeon had recommended I take a strong antibiotic the day before surgery which severely upset my stomach. Papa kindly sat up with me late into the night.

Surgery went well, but because one lymph node was malignant, chemotherapy was next on the list. Chemotherapy was something new to me back then and scary to think about, but sometimes one simply has to go forward. With God's help we made it through. The oncology nurses were wonderful. I didn't have a lot of side effects, but it seemed my stomach was unhappy a good deal of the time. Occasionally, I had a week off, and how wonderful I felt during those breaks!

Sometime that summer I wrote "My Cheer-Up Birds." While I was taking treatments, one of the other patients I talked with said, "Hope is like a dandelion. First a rabbit nibbles it, and then it is crushed underfoot." She did not say this in a bitter tone; I would guess she spoke from experience. I wanted a brighter ending to the analogy so I wrote "The Dandelion." Seven years later I can more deeply sympathize with the sentiments expressed by that lady whom I knew so briefly and never (to my knowledge) saw again. "God's Answer to Prayer" was written toward the end of that year.

I crossed off the treatments one by one. Slowly THE LAST DAY approached--December 26, 2001. How nice to think of being well again!

In the meantime Papa, who had been successfully treated for bladder cancer in 1992, was told the cancer had returned. At first we thought it was just in the bladder, but further testing showed it was in one kidney. He had that kidney removed in December. Now it was my turn to sit for several hours in suspense while a dear one was on the operating table. (One thing about being the patient yourself--you can sleep during the surgery!) Papa came through the surgery amazingly well, but the doctor did not have good news for us. He had removed the kidney and some lymph nodes, but the cancer was too involved for him to remove it all. It was a dreary day, and Kathy took me for another chemotherapy treatment that afternoon.

My treatments were barely over when Papa began his. Surprisingly, Papa's chemotherapy seemed to temporarily get rid of his cancer, and he was up and working nearly like usual that summer. I was feeling wonderfully well and happy. Never before had I appreciated my health so much.

But late in October my CEA (tumor marker) was elevated. More tests, more suspense. It was a sunny afternoon in November when the doctor called with the results from the CT scan. He said the cancer had showed up on the liver--one or two small spots. I asked him if having a liver resection was a possibility. "Oh, yes," he said, "we should consider it."

More chemotherapy. More tests. The doctor talked like the resection would not be an option if there was cancer anywhere else, and so much seemed to hinge on that surgery! It seemed like I was walking a narrow path along a cliff, and I never knew when the path would end in a drop off. I remember walking (for exercise) around the cider mill on frosty, starlit evenings, reminding myself of God's love and care. "On the Sea of Ill Health" was written sometime that winter. "Trust" was written on a day we were waiting for the results of one of Papa's tests, and that one did turn out well. What thankfulness!

And my tests were also turning out well; my tumor was shrinking and no cancer showed up anywhere else. We talked about surgery, but somehow we couldn't seem to make progress on plans. Then suddenly things fell into place. On February 27, 2003, a surgeon in South Bend removed twenty per cent of my liver. Although we had our anxious times, all in all the surgery and hospital stay went well. I didn't even have to have a blood transfusion. The tumor was encapsulated and the margins were clear. In just five days I was home, and, as usual, being thoroughly spoiled by my caring family.

Just before my surgery, John B. Martin contacted me concerning the poem "God's Answer to Prayer." He had seen it in a magazine and asked for permission to publish it with a tune of his own in his songbook. That was a nice diversion to think about!

That summer I had 12 chemotherapy treatments. A new drug was added to the list which made me more sick for a few days after each treatment. However, for a few days then I usually felt really well. The LAST DAY was July 22, and soon I was able to work almost as hard as ever.

Papa had a good spring and early summer. It was a pleasure to have him looking and acting so strong and healthy. Then on several occasions he had chest pains, and he had single bypass surgery in September. Later that fall a tumor the size of a quarter showed up in Papa's bladder. After all the cancer Papa and I had conquered in the last several years, that didn't sound too scary. More treatments, and at last we thought we might have clear sailing for a little while.

Papa was able to help with maple syrup season in 2004, but after that his cancer showed up again. More chemotherapy. In April he began having other symptoms; weak spells, headaches, vomiting...

That was a hard time because we knew those things were not good signs. More tests. Great suspense. On May 12, 2004, the doctor told us Papa had tumors on the brain. Papa began at once to take steroids to reduce the swelling, and it was like seeing a miracle! Suddenly he was very energetic and talkative. He took radiation treatments which went well for him.

But afterwards...in July he had a hard seizure, and from then on he gradually talked less and less. He soon required more care as walking became difficult. We did not spend as much time at our jobs away from home that summer, and we were able to get off as we felt we were needed at home. Our custom cider pressing was significantly less because of new FDA regulations. How glad we were for extra time to spend with Papa! He had taught us by example that there is a real blessing in assuming the care of one's parents, and we are so very, very thankful we were able to care for him.

At times he seemed stronger and would talk more, and we were happy to have him more alert. Later in October it became evident that he would not be with us long. We felt surrounded by the love and concern of friends and relatives.

The last several weeks I remember as a quiet and meaningful time though filled with sadness. Papa said little, but he knew us until a few days before his death. We were so thankful that he had a good appetite up to that time. We would usually take him to the table for dinner and supper, and I had the pleasure of feeding him. Toward the last we stayed in or near the house as much as possible. A couple evenings before he died, the Northern lights were more vivid and beautiful than any we children had ever seen.

All of us were at his bedside when Papa passed away peacefully on November 9, 2004. Several weeks earlier Ruthie had asked me to write a poem for his funeral. I didn't like doing it while he was still alive, but after his death we were so busy with funeral preparations, I could see the wisdom in doing it ahead of time.

In looking ahead to life without Papa, I imagined an extremely sad and dreary existence. But God is good, and though there was sadness in the months following the funeral, there was wonderful comfort, too. Suddenly heaven was a real place, not just something one read about and believed in. It was easy to think of Papa as only "gone on before."

The summer of 2005 was a pleasant one. All of us were home more than usual, and it was so nice to all be together. I had great fun working outside with Sam, learning new skills and feeling wonderfully well and strong.

During the fall and winter my tumor marker wavered about in the worry zone. The CT scans of my abdomen and pelvis were clear, but in April the CEA rose to the point where we were no longer comfortable. After a CT scan of my abdomen, pelvis, and chest on May 8, we learned there was a tumor in the upper lobe of my left lung on May 10, exactly 5 years after I had received the results of my first CT scan.

Somehow the diagnosis was harder for me to accept this time. I was thankful for the lessons learned in my previous cancer experiences, but I didn't want to return to being sick. Would I ever be well again? At my sisters' suggestion I had written "A Prayer for Healing," suitable for an anointing service. Now when I asked to be anointed again, we couldn't bring ourselves to use the song, fearing our tears would silence our singing.

More tests and consultations and plans for another surgery. One evening as I was packing things for my hospital stay, my uncle called. He had the poem "Highway of Our God," and he read some of it to me over the phone. It's one thing to write meaningful pieces; it's another to live it! But I really appreciated Uncle Harvey's concern, and it pleased me to know that he liked the poem.

I had surgery on May 24, 2006. I had worried that having half of one lung removed might severely limit my singing so I started to sing while still in ICU. I was home in less than a week, and my recovery was more speedy this time. However, the after effects have been more pronounced. I still have to be careful not to pull or lift an excessive amount with my left arm. Before surgery my lung capacity had been extra good so I get along fine even though it seems to be somewhat reduced.

Within a month I was taking chemotherapy again, 12 treatments, one every two weeks. The first several days after a treatment, Ruthie and the others would faithfully give me my anti-nausea medicine which made me sleep much of the time. After that the nausea usually wasn't too bad.

As the weeks wore on, I experienced more depression on the third day after the treatment. It was not a pleasant feeling, to state it mildly. Normally I enjoy reading immensely, but I would sit there with a book in my hands and discover I wasn't reading. I would refocus on the words only to find my mind wandering in a few minutes. The next day usually was better, and the day after that I would be in pretty good spirits. On one of my sick days someone who had taken the same kind of treatment stopped by. He came in to meet me and reassured me that it was the drugs that caused the depression. That was comforting to know!

November 20 was another LAST DAY I was so very happy to see arrive. CT scans turned out well. Although my CEA was within normal limits, we wished it would have been lower. Still there was much to be thankful for, and I hoped for a few good years at least. Maybe if the cancer did return, there would be new weapons with which to meet it. I was ready to be well and to be Sam's right-hand helper the next summer.

First, though, I had to recover from my ordeal. This took rather longer this time, but thankfully the nausea and depression quickly disappeared. "What Life Is About" reflects my struggle with impatience to be doing the many things which had been pushed back during my illness.

I remember so well the day in March when I was finally getting "back to it" again. It was unseasonably warm, and Sam, Becky, and I were making firewood in the lower pasture. I had great fun splitting short lengths for the greenhouse stove and even took some licks at the longer pieces for the stove in the house. Then I started having pain on my left side. Well, I sheepishly agreed that perhaps it was too much for my arm to use it so strenuously. I had a routine CT scan and CEA near the end of March. The CEA was too high...oh, not again! and so soon!

The doctor was kind but honest. The scans showed fluid on my left lung and a few nodules which, with the rising CEA, certainly indicated cancer. No, surgery was not an option, but with chemotherapy he expected me to be around awhile yet. It was not until we were on the way home that the truth began to soak in. I tried to take a nap after dinner, but I ended up crying instead of sleeping. My dear family rallied around and encouraged me as best they could.

It was harder than ever this time to accept the diagnosis and prognosis. By this time I was sick of being sick. Besides, after losing Papa, it was hard to think of the others facing a fresh bereavement so soon. I had tried to assume in a small way some of Papa's duties, and to think of the rest struggling on without me was enough to make me want to cry.

Early in 2006, when I had written "It Takes a Lot of Courage" for a young friend whose cancer had returned, I had been in excellent health, and I thought perhaps the poem made the struggle with cancer sound a bit harder than it really was. Now, however, as I reread the poem, I realized it fit better than I had imagined. I learned then that even though I had been through it before, remembering it is still not like living it.

More tests. More suspense. More consultations. We saw another oncologist and he said basically what the first one had said; chemotherapy was the only treatment and there was no cure. I was not ready to think of standard chemotherapy at that point, not if there were any other options. It was at this point I decided to get serious about the poem book. And how could Ruthie say no to her "little" sister under such circumstances?

Through a health magazine we learned of the Burzynski Clinic in Texas. Dr. Burzynski specializes in peptide therapy, but he does use additional anti-cancer therapies for some of his patients. I likely would not have paid a lot of attention to the article, but a highly-respected friend of the family also pointed it out to us. It sounded good, and yet not too good to be true. We had never dreamed we'd go out on a limb like that, but one never knows what one will do when one gets desperate. How we prayed about it! and the doors seemed to open up for us to go.

On April 19, 2007, Mama, Sam, and I left for Texas. Thankfully, I was feeling pretty well. I think it was hard for my sisters to see me go.

We decided we might as well enjoy the trip which in itself was a novelty. On the whole we were well impressed with the clinic and convinced that, while it was no quick and easy miracle cure, it was no scam either. The doctors could not promise me I would be cured, but they talked like there certainly was hope. "A Thank You to My Friends" was written while we were in Texas.

We arrived home on May 5. I had a lot of pills to take: the peptide therapy, some supplements, gene targeted therapy drugs, and oral chemotherapy. My medicine has been changed or adjusted a number of times since then. I frequently talk with staff from the clinic over the telephone. I have PET scans taken at local facilities, and the results are sent to the clinic. The radiologist at Burzynski's also reads the scans, and I have access to both reports. Blood draws are done at my family doctor's office. He and his staff are more than medical professionals; they are friends. This also can be said of many of the other doctors and nurses I have had during these last seven years.

On May 3, my CEA had been 84. On May 10, it had dropped to 22. Although that was still well above normal limits, the news that it had dropped so much was thrilling! It continued to drop, but more slowly, for several weeks. The PET scan in June showed no cancer in the lungs. Then the CEA began to rise a bit, and the PET scan in September showed cancer activity again. What a disappointment!

Since that time it has been an up-and-down thing. Sometimes, like in January when another PET scan was clear, it looks hopeful. Another scan in May showed a little cancer activity again. I have felt fairly well a good bit of the time since starting this treatment. (Actually, at the time of this writing in August, I am delighted to be feeling nearly as good as ever, though I am not ready to start splitting wood.) Usually I have been well enough to help Sam milk the cow in the evenings, and that has been good therapy for me. Mama and Becky appreciate my help in the house. I've always had plenty of things to do to fit my level of energy. During my tired times I sleep more during the day which sometimes upsets my sleeping pattern. I wrote (or began composing) "He Giveth His Beloved Sleep" late one wakeful night.

My cancer is not as easy for doctors at the clinic in Texas to target as some kinds are, and the hope that their medicine can cure me has become more faint. Still, we are glad we went to the Burzynski Clinic because it seems remarkable that I am doing as well as I am. This has been a blessing while writing the poem book because at times with earlier treatments I was unable to concentrate very well.

How will my battle with cancer end? "God knoweth the future; we live day by day," * is a phrase which comes to mind when that question raises itself. Writing "My HOME by the River" and the Beatitude poems during the last several months has been good for me; it has made me ponder anew the beauties of heaven and the joy of seeing God face to face. But whatever happens, it is such a comfort to believe in "[God's] grace that, when needed, will always be here." *

--Mary E. Miller 2008

* My Home by the River
* Beatitude Poem No. 8; Matthew 5:10-12

Are not two sparrows sold for a farthing? and one of them shall not fall on the ground without your Father. But the very hairs of your head are all numbered. Fear ye not therefore, ye are of more value than many sparrows.
Matthew 10:29-31

It Takes a Lot of Courage

by Mary E. Miller

It takes a lot of courage
  Just to start another day
With all of its uncertainties
  Which tempt one to dismay.
When persistent, plaguing questions
  Keep knock, knocking at your heart,
Yes, it takes a lot of courage
  Just to give the day a start.

It takes a lot of patience
  Just to see this long thing through,
When the days before your illness
  Seem a distant dream to you,
When the doctors keep you waiting
  With their tests and tests and tests,
And you feel the nagging worries
  Which your weary mind suggests.

It takes a lot of trusting
  To believe God works things out
For the best when you are tempted
  With discouragement and doubt,
To believe that for each moment
  Ample grace will be supplied
And to long for, more than healing,
  That the Lord be glorified.

But it is when we are weakest
  God can make us to be strong.
He can make us brave and patient
  When the trial stretches long.
And it is when life is blackest
  In affliction's lonely night
That we see with clearest vision
  The bright glory of His light.

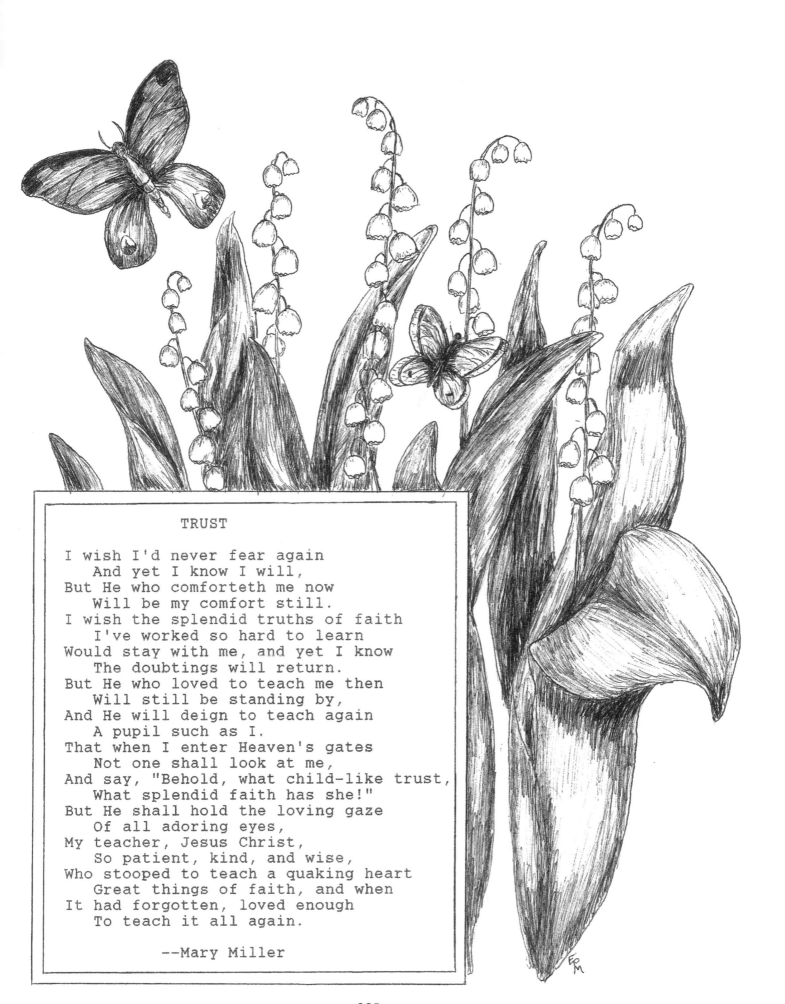

TRUST

I wish I'd never fear again
   And yet I know I will,
But He who comforteth me now
   Will be my comfort still.
I wish the splendid truths of faith
   I've worked so hard to learn
Would stay with me, and yet I know
   The doubtings will return.
But He who loved to teach me then
   Will still be standing by,
And He will deign to teach again
   A pupil such as I.
That when I enter Heaven's gates
   Not one shall look at me,
And say, "Behold, what child-like trust,
   What splendid faith has she!"
But He shall hold the loving gaze
   Of all adoring eyes,
My teacher, Jesus Christ,
   So patient, kind, and wise,
Who stooped to teach a quaking heart
   Great things of faith, and when
It had forgotten, loved enough
   To teach it all again.

                    --Mary Miller

239

Likewise the Spirit also helpeth our infirmities: for we know not what we should pray for as we ought: but the Spirit itself maketh intercession for us with groanings which cannot be uttered. And he that searcheth the hearts knoweth what is the mind of the Spirit, because he maketh intercession for the saints according to the will of God.   And we know that all things work together for good to them that love God, to them who are the called according to his purpose. Romans 8:26-28

He shall not be afraid of evil tidings: his heart is fixed, trusting in the Lord. Psalm 112:7

I can do all things through Christ which strengtheneth me. Philippians 4:13

Thou therefore endure hardness, as a good soldier of Jesus Christ. II Timothy 2:3

My times are in thy hand: Psalm 31:15a

...Weeping may endure for a night, but joy cometh in the morning. Psalm 30:5

But he knoweth the way that I take: when he hath tried me, I shall come forth as gold. Job 23:10

What time I am afraid, I will trust in thee. Psalm 56:3

Bless the Lord, O my soul: and all that is within me, bless his holy name. Who forgiveth all thine iniquities; who healeth all thy diseases; For as the heaven is high above the earth, so great is his mercy toward them that fear him. Psalm 103:1, 3 & 11

Cast thy burden upon the Lord, and he shall sustain thee: he shall never suffer the righteous to be moved. Psalm 55:22

Hear my cry, O God; attend unto my prayer. From the end of the earth will I cry unto thee, when my heart is overwhelmed: lead me to the rock that is higher than I. Psalm 61:1&2

Be merciful unto me, O God, be merciful unto me: for my soul trusteth in thee: yea, in the shadow of thy wings will I make my refuge, until these calamities be overpast. Psalm 57:1

Thou wilt keep him in perfect peace, whose mind is stayed on thee: because he trusteth in thee. Isaiah 26:3

The eternal God is thy refuge, and underneath are the everlasting arms: Deuteronomy 33:27a

A Prayer for Healing

(May be sung to the tune of,
"I heard the Voice of Jesus say,"
or, "There Is a Land of Pure Delight.")

Oh, Lord, Thou knowest very well
    The cause of our distress--
The failing health, the dread disease,
    And our own helplessness.
Our hearts are burdened, yet we sing
    In our extremity.
For courage, healing, help, and hope
    Oh, Lord, we come to Thee.

It was Thy great and mighty pow'r
    This body did create.
No sickness is too hard for Thee,
    No miracle too great.
Though medicine is limited,
    And doctors are unsure,
It only takes one word from Thee
    To work a perfect cure.

Yet more than this we ask of Thee
    A holy, inner peace
Which makes all bitter thoughts depart
    And worryings to cease,
Which knows that all-sufficient grace
    Will day by day be given,
And looks beyond the raging storm
    Into the face of heaven.

Oh, Lord, Thy holy will be done!
    We crave this most of all.
Then we shall find the promised joy
    Whatever may befall.
Sometimes we know not what to pray
    Nor always what is best,
But ev'ry prayer which ends this way
    Will leave us safe and blest.

--Mary E. Miller

The Dandelion

Among the fresh, green blades of grass
  A dandelion grew.
The frilly petals on his head
  Were thick and bright and new.
He proudly held his head erect
  As if to say, "Behold,
How like a king of flow'rs am I
  Thus decked and crowned with gold!"
A rabbit saw him growing there
  And snatched a hurried bite.
He quickly lost his kingly air
  But was not ruined, quite.
There came a laughing, barefoot child
  Beneath whose dancing feet
The stem was bent. The head was crushed.
  The ruin was complete.
Ah, whisper to the sturdy plant
  That mourns the missing face,
"Another flower soon will grow
  To fill the vacant place.
"Your roots grow deeply in the soil.
  Your leaves absorb the sun.
Although 'tis sad the flower died
  Your work is not yet done."

Alas, how oft our cherished dreams
  Are ruined, crushed, and dead.
For fragile dreams cannot be safe
  Where disappointments tread.
If we are rooted in God's Word
  And basking in His light,
How strong our confidence may be
  That all will turn out right!
Our disappointments can be used
  By God to cleanse our souls
Of selfish dreams, of petty aims,
  Of earthy, short-ranged goals.
To love and serve and trust the Lord
  No matter what befall
Is one great goal, the highest aim,
  The sweetest dream of all!
                    --Mary Miller

What Life is About

My life is not about myself,
    My hopes, my plans, my dreams,
My selfish longings and desires,
    My self-exalting schemes.
It's all about the will of God
    And showing forth His praise.
Have I not said that they are His--
    My life, my heart, my days?
As long as I remember this
    It smooths away the stress,
For I can trust the Lord to bring
    His plans to good success.
He will endow me with enough
    Of time and strength and skill,
And wisdom, health, and energy
    To do my Master's will.
But I confess with shame-filled heart
    How often I forget!
And as I watch my ruined plans,
    I fume and fuss and fret.
So as I face each brand-new day
    A helpful motto is,
"Remember I am not my own,
    My life, my all, are His."
          --Mary E. Miller

Highway of Our God

If our God would fill the valleys
 And would bring the mountains low
As a literal fulfillment
 Of the words penned long ago,
What a smooth and level pathway
 With its course so clear and plain,
And how easy to traverse it
 With no obstacles or pain!

But our God does greater wonders,
 For we find our valleys filled
With His kindly love and comfort,
 And our fears are hushed and stilled.
He can pour a strength upon us
 Just a portion for each hour,
And our mountain stands beneath us
 Conquered by God's mighty pow'r.

If we ask the Lord for wisdom
 And with trusting patience wait,
He will show the step before us.
 Thus He makes the crooked straight.
When the way is hard and rocky,
 God can smooth the roughest place
With the wonder of His presence
 And the beauty of His grace.

If our eyes had not beheld them--
 Valleys, hills, and crooked ways,
And His wonderful deliv'rance--
 Would our hearts be filled with praise?
And our faith, unused, unneeded,
 Would become weak, faint, and dim.
For the object of our journey
 Is to draw us close to Him.
                    --Mary E. Miller

God's Answer To Prayer

Mary E. Miller

John B. Martin

1. When we ap - peal to God in our dis - tress, And He in
2. But when His an - swer is a "No," or "Wait," Do we re -
3. He doth not will - ing - ly af - flict all men. That He al -
4. And will - ing - ly o - bey His Word and will, And in all

kind - ness prompt - ly an - swers, "Yes," How we ex - tol Him for His
spond with thank - ful - ness as great? God's care is just as car - ing
lows this tri - al must mean, then, It com - eth not to vex, but
cir - cum - stan - ces trust Him still. Then wheth - er "No," or "Wait a

lov - ing care! What sweet as - sur - ance that He an - swers prayer!
as be - fore; His love is just as lov - ing, may - be more.
for our good, If we but learn to love Him as we should.
while," or "Yes," All an - swers mean e - ven - tual hap - pi - ness.

67

To My Nurse

For all the extra pains you take,

For all the extra calls you make,

And all the time you spend,

For all the the things you do for me

I thank you with sincerity,

My more than nurse,

my friend.

M.E.M.

A Thank You to My Friends

Some brought good food. Some sent a card.
    One brought a fragrant rose.
How many asked about my health
    No human being knows.
Some wanted to be notified
    If they could render aid.
Some called and chatted on the phone,
    And many, many prayed.
Some wrote kind notes. Some folks dropped in.
    Some helped financially.
Much time and effort were put forth
    And all because of me!
It makes me feel so very loved
    Yet somehow rather small.
How could I cope if I believed
    I must repay it all?
Receiving all these gifts of love
    Has meant so much to me,
And givers are more greatly blessed--
    Christ said that they would be.
My heart is warmed and greatly cheered
    By what our friends have done.
So let me say with gratitude,
    "I thank you, ev'ry one!"

                                    --Mary E. Miller

He Giveth His Beloved Sleep
Psalm 127:2

The hurried bustle of the day
Must in the silence fade away.
Tomorrow's cares will surely keep.
God giveth His beloved sleep.

The nagging worries, large and small,
The Lord looks down and sees them all,
The caring Shepherd loves His sheep.
He giveth His beloved sleep.

When threat of danger hovers near,
When hearts are filled with anxious fear,
God is awake to guard and keep
And watch while His beloved sleep.

When grief is real and fresh and new,
If sorrow long has walked with you,
God comforts all His saints that weep
And gives to His beloved sleep.

Sometimes the night grows wearisome.
It seems that sleep will never come!
If we but knew how God can bless
The hours of patient wakefulness.

Sometimes the darkness of the night
Can show more clearly wrong from right.
The voice of conscience speaks within
And we confess to God our sin.

What prayers for others can be said
By those who keep a sleepless bed!
Sometimes in mem'ry's ear is heard
A precious passage from God's word.

And when the hours stretch dark and long,
God gives the melody of song.
At length He will His promise keep
And give to His beloved sleep.

--Mary Elaine Miller

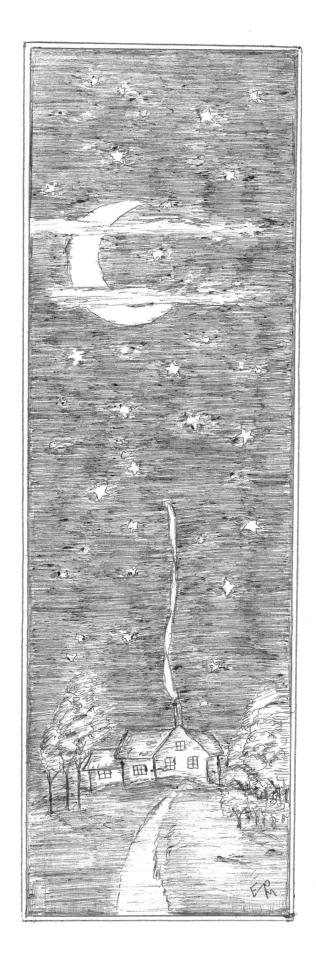

Chapter Eleven

WISDOM FROM THE BIBLE

The sheep grazing in the pasture

II Timothy III

16.　All scripture is given by inspiration of God, and is profitable for doctrine, for reproof, for correction, for instruction in righteousness:

17.　That the man of God may be perfect, throughly furnished unto all good works.

And God saw everything that He made...

And It Was Good

In the beginning of the world
    When all the earth in chaos stood
God spoke. He said, "Let there be light."
    God spoke. It was. And it was good.

God spoke. The firmament appeared,
    Dry land and plants, the stars and sun,
The fish and fowl and animals.
    God spoke the word and it was done.

How great and mighty is God's word!
    The natural things at once obey
And all is well and all is good
    Where God can fully have His way.

Today God's word is speaking yet.
    But God has given man the choice
And will or will he not obey
    The clear directives of God's voice?

Oh, that in countries far and near
    This truth were clearly understood,
All those who heed God's Word will find
    That all is well, and all is good.
              -Mary E. Miller

251

The Israelites

When the Israelites cried unto God in distress,
  God rendered a mighty salvation.
They went out from Egypt with goods in excess--
  A thankful and jubilant nation.

They came to the Red Sea and stood on its coast
  Where the camps of all Israel assembled.
Egyptians pursued them--a dangerous host!
  With terror and fear Israel trembled.

Again God delivered with powerful arm.
  The waters fell back and divided,
And Israel escaped without capture or harm.
  Their fears and their tremblings subsided.

The water of Marah, too bitter to drink,
  Caused many to cry against Moses.
Why did they all panic? Why didn't they think?
  God accomplishes what He proposes.

Over and over it happened again
  As Moses recorded the story
The testings, the bitter complainings, and then
  Deliverance showing God's glory.

It wasn't the sea in the way as they fled,
  It wasn't the army pursuing,
It wasn't the need of the water and bread,
  That proved to be Israel's undoing,

But unbelief prompted the Lord to withhold
  The joys He delights in bestowing.
And for our improvement He caused to be told
  The story that's well worth our knowing.

It isn't the size of the trials we face
  That causes the fear and the pouting.
It's failing to realize the depth of God's grace
  And unbelief, fearing, and doubting.

                              --Mary E. Miller

252

Radiant Beams

When Gideon and his small handful of men
    Surrounded the Midian's camp,
Each Israelite had a trumpet to blow
    And a pitcher concealing a lamp.

Though each of those lamps may have burned very well
    No ray pierced the gloom of the night,
For not till the pitchers were broken were seen
    The lamps with their flickering light.

Oh, God, when the heart which Thy Spirit has touched
    With the glorious breath of Thy flame,
Has let its own wilfulness largely conceal
    The light which would honor Thy name;

Then blest be the circumstance, trial, or pain,
    The thwarting of self and its dreams,
Which breaks all the wilful resistance away
    Revealing God's radiant beams.

-Mary E. Miller

John X

14. I am the good shepherd, and know my sheep, and am known of mine.
15. As the Father knoweth me, even so know I the Father: and I lay down my life for the sheep.
16. And other sheep I have, which are not of this fold: them also I must bring, and they shall hear my voice; and there shall be one fold, and one shepherd.

Psalm 23:1

I shall not want for anything
    Because my Shepherd is the Lord.
Cannot our God, the Sovereign King
    Of all the universe, afford
To give His own all they require?
    And then because He loves me so,
And I love Him, shall I desire
    The thing to which His Word says, "No"?
And if some blessings, good and right,
    He chooses to withhold from me,
Can He not teach me to delight
    In His sweet will, whate'er it be?
And though the tears of sorrow fall,
    And disappointment leaves its scar,
God's ways are best. He sees it all.
    How great His ways and workings are!
                --Mary E. Miller

The Lord is my shepherd; I shall not want.

Psalm 23:2

Where green grow the grasses,
　　Where pastures are lush,
My soul lies protected
　　From life's hectic rush.
My hands may be busy
　　And hurried my feet,
But love for my Master
　　Makes duty seem sweet.
No pride or peer pressure
　　Shall add to my tasks,

If I do His bidding--
　　Whatever He asks.
Beside the still waters
　　He leadeth the way.
No dryness of thirstings
　　Shall cause me dismay.
His Spirit is water.
　　His Word is my bread.
Abundantly, daily
　　I'm watered and fed.

--Mary E. Miller

He maketh me to lie down in green pastures: he leadeth me beside the still waters.

Psalm 23:3

My shepherd is lovingly watching my steps.
    No part of my life He ignoreth.
When threatened by danger, discouraged, distressed,
    My soul He in pity restoreth.

The path which looks easy and pleasant to me
    He sees from beginning to ending.
He sees how deceitfully quickly it turns
    To evil and ruin descending.

And so for the sake of His own blessed Name,
    My trust and obedience pleading,
He goeth before and He calls me to come
    In pathways of righteousness leading.

--Mary E. Miller

He restoreth my soul: he leadeth me in the paths of righteousness for his name's sake.

Psalm 23:4

To walk through the vale of the shadow of death
    Alone would cause horrible fear.
My Shepherd goes with me. What comfort to know
    His powerful presence is near!

I do not know whether this pathway will lead
    To safety when danger is past,
Or if it will lead to the City of God,
    My wanderings ended at last.

Whatever may happen, my Shepherd will use
    His comforting staff and His rod.
With love and with wisdom. Oh, how I shall sing
    The wonderful goodness of God!

          --Mary E. Miller

Yea, though I walk through the valley of the shadow of death, I will fear no evil: for thou art with me; thy rod and thy staff they comfort me.

Psalm 23:5

While my enemies are watching,
   I sit down where Thou hast spread
Food in plenty on the table;
   And Thou pourest on my head
Oil which smoothes the petty troubles,
   Those frustrations which annoy.
And my cup is running over
   With a glad and thankful joy.

--Mary E. Miller

Thou preparest a table before me in the presence of mine enemies: thou anointest my head with oil; my cup runneth over.

Psalm 23:6

My Shepherd is good.
    His mercy is great.
I follow His footsteps
    In the way that is strait.
It follows therefore
    (How else could it be?)
That goodness and mercy
    Are following me.

His way is not aimless.
    We do not just roam.
My Shepherd has asked me
    To come to His Home.
It cheers me as onward
    And onward I plod
To think of our Home
    And Forever with God.
        --Mary E. Miller

Surely goodness and mercy shall follow me all the days of my life: and I will dwell in the house of the LORD forever.

The Beatitudes

And seeing the multitudes, he went up into a mountain: and when he was set, his disciples came unto him: And he opened his mouth, and taught them, saying, Matthew 5:1 & 2.

Blessed are the poor in spirit,
    Those who keenly feel
That they have no self-earned merit,
    And whose hearts appeal
Unto Christ to freely bless
    With His boundless grace
That His perfect righteousness
    Might their own replace.

Unto them shall there be given
Of the kingdom of God's heaven.

Righteous kingdom, blest and holy.
Father, make me humble, lowly.

--Mary Elaine Miller

262

Blessed are those that mourn.
    Blessed are they who weep,
Whose weary hearts have been torn
    By the tempests of guilt that sweep.

Blessed are they who have known
    The reason for which Christ came,
Who trust in His blood alone
    And honor His holy name.

What wonderful comfort they feel,
    Rejoicing with laughter and song.

Lord Jesus, hear Thou my appeal,
    Oh, save me from sin and from wrong.

--Mary Elaine Miller

Blessed are the meek,
    The ones who are willing to learn,
Those who pray'rfully seek
    The will of God to discern,
And, finding that will, shall rest
    No matter what trials unfold,
Trusting the fiery test
    Will make them come forth as gold.
And they that truly are meek
    Will conquer their fellowmen
By turning the other cheek,
    Forgiving again and again.

For they shall inherit the earth.
    The Father most freely shall bless,
Remem'bring their spiritual birth
    Shall give them all things to possess.

Lord, teach me to suffer with joy
    And trustfully rest in Thy will,
When fellowmen irk and annoy,
    To treat them with patient goodwill.

--Mary Elaine Miller

264

Blessed are they which do hunger and thirst after righteousness: for they shall be filled. Matthew 5:6

Blessed are they which do hunger and thirst
    And long after righteousness,
Those who seek always God's kingdom things first
    The pearl of great price to possess.

For they shall be filled, like children be fed,
Christ's crucified body their heavenly bread.
The milk of God's Word or wholesome, strong meat,
A daily provision shall they have to eat.
A river of waters shall spring from the well
In hearts where God's spirit consenteth to dwell.

Lord, grant me that hunger and teach me to feed
On spiritual manna which filleth indeed.

             --Mary Elaine Miller

Blessed are the merciful
    Which show a kind compassion,
Who seek to touch the sin-sick soul
    In Christ-like, loving fashion.

For mercy shall they obtain.
    When Judgment shall sit on the throne,
Those merciful deeds shall remain
    And Christ shall acknowledge His own.
While yet on the earth they shall know
    New blessings of mercy each day.
Its fountain unceasing shall flow
    Encompassing them with its spray.

Oh, God, may I lavishly, freely impart
The mercy Thy kindness has taught to my heart.

            --Mary Elaine Miller

266

Blessed are the pure in heart,
Those who draw themselves apart
    From defiling sin and evil wrong.
Those who look to Christ for keeping
When temptation's blasts are sweeping,
Christ Who is no more found sleeping,
    Christ Who calms the storm and makes them strong.

For they shall see God.
    A Presence divine
Shall ever go with them
    And inwardly shine,
Shall temple Himself
    In hearts that are pure,
Shall render a joy
    And confidence sure.
Not even death's coming
    This union shall sever;
God's pure ones shall see Him
    Forever and ever.

Oh, Jesus, beholding the joy of Thy face,
Renews me with patience to run in the race,
Refreshes my courage to lay sins aside,
Allowing my heart to be cleansed, purified.
Oh, may this sustain me as onward I plod,
The thought of beholding the face of my God.

—Mary Elaine Miller

Blessed are the peacemakers,
　　Those who spread a calm
Over angry, wounded souls
　　Like a healing balm,
Those who let no selfish whim
　　Ever interfere
With the peace of brotherhood
　　Which they hold so dear,
They who know that compromise
　　With the downward trend
Makes a truce that only proves
　　Fleeting in the end,
They whose feet with Gospel peace
　　Day by day are shod,
They who help a fellowman
　　Find his peace with God.

For they shall be called the children of God.
　　No title of earthly fame,
No recognition the world can give
　　Can rival the joy of that name.
The children of God!　His daughters and sons!
　　This honor shall never cease
For they with their Father forever shall dwell
　　In heaven, God's kingdom of peace.

Submission, obedience--liberty's choice,
　　(My self would be far more demanding.)
When following Jesus, my heart shall rejoice
　　In peace that is past understanding.
May others, observing this wondrous release,
Be led to my Savior, my Lord, Prince of Peace.

　　　　　　　　　　--Mary Elaine Miller

Blessed are the persecuted
    For the sake of righteousness,
Whom the Father has recruited
    Of His glory to profess.
Who endure the jeers and jibings,
    Sneers, reproaches, flame, or sword,
Who cannot be moved by bribings,
    All because they love the Lord.

For theirs is the kingdom of heaven.
To them a reward shall be given,
White-robed and exultant, triumphant, rejoicing,
The praises of God and the Lamb ever voicing.
And even before this life's journey is done,
Their role of rejoicing is gladly begun.

Lord, help me remember those prisoned and bound
    Or dying for Thee or reviled.
I know I am blest if my pray'rs may be found,
    Upholding the strength of Thy child.
And may I remember that if I am called
    As worthy to suffer Thy shame,
My heart may be steady, my faith unappalled,
    The stores of Thy grace I may claim.
Thy grace all sufficient, Thy grace ever near,
Thy grace that, when needed, will always be here.

                --Mary Elaine Miller

Giving All

When Jesus fed the multitude,
    It seems the little lad
Had given all his simple lunch,
    Yes, ev'ry bit he had.

If he had kept back for himself
    One little loaf of bread,
Could he have watched with such delight
    The hungry being fed?

If that poor widow with two mites
    Had cast in only one,
Would Christ have said those words to praise
    The act which she has done?

Those gifts, the fish, the loaves, the mites,
    Were really very small,
But Christ could bless and feed and praise,
    For they had given all.

God knows the purpose of each heart.
    He sees the true intent.
It matters not how great the gift
    But only what percent.

--Mary E. Miller

The Life of Christ

--Mary E. Miller

The story of Jesus is known to us all.
Let's pause to remember and fondly recall
Events of his lifetime, beginning with when
He came as a baby to dwell among men.
The birth in the stable, the song in the night,
The wise men who followed the star's guiding light.

The story continues--in stature He grew,
In wisdom, in favor with God and man, too.
We read of the blind man whose sight was restored,
And many diseases were healed by the Lord.
When children came to Him for blessing one day,
He told His disciples, "Don't send them away.
Suffer the children to come unto me.
Of such is the kingdom of heaven," said He.
Whoever His list'ners wherever He trod,
He constantly pointed the people to God.

One night in the garden He wrestled in pray'r.
His helpers were sleeping. None watched with Him there.
But God sent His angels to strengthen His Son.
Christ said, "Oh, My Father, may Thy will be done!"
Our Lord was betrayed and by Peter denied.
It was for the sins of the whole world He died.
But after three days the glad tidings were spread,
"Our Lord hath arisen again from the dead!"

He suffered so greatly for you and for me.
The gift of salvation, how wondrously free!
It's up to each one of us now to decide
If we will accept His great gifts and abide
Within His sweet will and His teaching obey
To travel with Him on the strait, narrow way.

How Jesus came down to this earth long ago
Is a wonderful story and one we all know.
He says in His Word He is coming again
To judge by their actions the nations of men.
All those who are faithfully watching with pray'r
Will rise up to heaven to dwell with Him there.

Palm Sunday

The people in the noisy throng
    Moved down the dusty track
With Jesus in the midst of them
    Upon the donkey's back.
And when they came to where the mount
    Begins its steep descent,
They took the branches of green palms
    And waved them as they went.
The branches and their garments, too,
    They strawed upon the way
To show with what a high regard
    They held the Lord that day.
Oh, how they cried with joyful voice
    And made the echoes ring,
"Hosanna unto David's son!
    Hosanna to the King!
To Him who came in God's own Name
    Great blessings shall be given;
May glory in the highest be
    And peace abide in heaven!"

It's likely not a one of them
    Who shouted joyously
Once thought of Zechariah
    And his words of prophecy,
Or dreamed long after people still
    Would read this brief account,
Of Jesus and the happy throng
    Who journeyed down the mount.
Or what a bright and pleasant scene
    The story would portray,
Or what a lesson it would teach
    To us who live today.
Oh, may our thoughts, our words, our deeds,
    Our lives forever bring
Great honor and unceasing praise
    To Jesus Christ our King!
                    --Mary E. Miller

The Thief on the Cross

Nothing of good in his record
   To use as a base for his claim,
Only a bad reputation,
   Only a thief's wretched name.

Nothing to draw from the future,
   Nothing to promise to give,
Only the horror of dying,
   Only some hours to live.

He knew and he felt he had nothing.
   The humbled and penitent thief
Saw Jesus had something eternal.
   He acted upon this belief.

He uttered his simple petition.
   Christ honored the outlaw's request.
His righteousness covered the sinner
   And gave him a future most blest.

--Mary E. Miller

Easter's Glad Song

How sad was Good Friday
    When death hovered near.
The band of disciples
    Was stricken with fear.

Their hopes for the freedom
    Christ promised to bring--
Their dreams of Christ reigning
    As Israel's King--

These dreams lay in ruins,
    Their hopes seemed in vain,
For Christ had been captured,
    Dishonored, and slain.

But then came the Easter,
    That wonderful day,
When joy was triumphant,
    And grief fled away!

For Christ had arisen!
    The wonder He wrought
Exceeded what mortals
    Had hoped, dreamed, and thought.

When sorrows surround us,
    When trials dismay,
When sadness has taken
    Our gladness away--

We then must remember
    God's wonderful plan
Exceeds ev'ry blessing
    Imagined by man.

Be faithful. Be patient.
    Be cheerful and strong,
For after Good Friday
    Comes Easter's glad song.

                --Mary Elaine Miller

274

Chapter Twelve

MESSAGES OF FAITH AND HOPE

Sunlight streaming down on the little island
with a miniature lighthouse

Then Go Thou Forth

The morning spreads its rays of hope and promise
    Upon the earth to wake it from its rest.
Then go thou forth to do thy Father's bidding
    With all thine energies, with all thy best.
Then when thine eyes shall see the setting sun,
Thy heart shall rest content in work well done.

The spring bursts forth with tender bud and blossom,
    Its hope and promise smile upon the land.
Then till the soil and plant thy fields and gardens
    With chosen seed and willing, careful hand.
Then if thy harvest lack full recompense
Thou shalt not charge thyself with indolence.

And youth is full of life and hope and promise
    With dreams and plans and energies aflame.
Then fail not thou to look to Heaven's teaching
    And make the Lord thy Master, God thine aim.
When age shall see the path thy life has trod,
Thy thankful soul shall rest itself in God.

--Mary E. Miller

YOUTH

To walk or run just as I please,
To hold my arms out to the breeze,
To look above to skies and trees,
   This is youth.

Buttons slip neatly where they belong.
To put my clothes on never takes long.
My voice is raised in steady song.
   Blessed youth.

Someday I'll struggle where'er I go.
The frustrations of dressing all I'll know.
My voice unsteady and shaky will grow.
   Ah, for youth.

But if I lend a hand along the way,
Trusting and serving God each day,
In His will obediently stay,
   What is youth?

Some day in heaven by His grace,
Looking into that blessed face,
Singing forever that song of praise,
   I'll have youth.

Immortal youth, which never grows old,
Praising untiringly that love untold,
Walking forever on streets of gold,
   Immortal youth.

--Kathleen J. Miller 1993

Sky Light and Shadow

Blue sky glory all the day,
Crystal clear, and far away;
Sparkling bright from side to side,
Not a shadow does it hide.
I love it all; and yet, and yet,
When skies are blue I soon forget,
To trust the mighty power of God
And leave His ways for paths untrod.

But when the day is dark and bleak
And for the path I vainly seek,
The storm clouds roll and heave their way
Across my world and seem to stay.
My feeble faith is almost lost,
And I am weary, temptest-tossed.
I turn to God and then I see
A blue-sky band in the west for me!

Somehow it means so much, much more,
That band of blue in the western door;
I'd never trade in any way
For blue-sky glory of yesterday.

The sun shines bright in living spring.
It softly calls each growing thing;
To its warm rays I turn my face
And gladly greet its fond embrace.
It's great! It's grand! and yet I know
That seasons come and seasons go.
Where now my world is bathed in light
Too soon the snow will blow at night.

But now unfolds before my eyes
A picture filled with sun-surprise!
It bids farewell to the world below
In dazzling colors the clouds do show.
Though grim and dark they mean to be,
Where sunlight plays I now can see
Colors and glories of orange and red
Until the last of light has fled.

I look beyond this sunset vision
And see almost the gates of heaven.
Though seasons here may come and go,
Eternal spring blooms there, I know!

Star-spangled wonder of the skies
I love to stand and raise my eyes.
On some clear night the moon has gone
And left the stars to gaze upon.
I see them near, I see them far.
Each time I turn, another star
Has burst into my world of vision
And sparkles on to fill its mission.

But then there comes a night so dark
I cannot see the faintest spark,
The moon and stars refuse to shine;
It almost smothers this heart of mine.
I stand at the brink of giving in,
Just letting go and turning to sin,
When far away from dark cloud lines,
One star bursts through and bravely shines!

It thrills me so, this little star;
It gleams of faith and love from far.
Though other stars forget their part,
This one shines on and warms my heart.
--Samuel A. Miller 1984

278

A PRAYER OF THE HEART

Give me a pure, clean heart.
   Cleansed from all sin may it be.
Washed and made white in the blood of the Lamb.
   Shining in purity.

Give me a trusting heart,
   Confident in Thy care.
Burdens of life I have laid at Thy feet.
   Teach me to leave them there.

Give me a thankful heart.
   Fill it with gratitude
For spiritual blessings that I have received
   And plenty of clothes and food.

Give me a joyful heart.
   Constant its source of delight--
Readiness only to do what is good
   And pleasing in Thy sight.

Give me a generous heart
   Willingly ready to share
Time, things and talents to help those in need
   And lighten the load they bear.

Give me a loving heart.
   Loving Thee first, and then
May all my thoughts and expressions and deeds
   Show love to my fellowmen.

Give me a cheerful heart,
   Bursting with happy song.
Knowing the wonderful joy of the Lord
   Is such as to make one strong.

Take then my heart, oh Lord,
   Work of Thy mercy and grace.
Now the most glorious crowning of all--
   Make it Thy dwelling place.
              --Mary E. Miller

Philippians IV

7. And the peace of God, which passeth all understanding, shall keep your hearts and minds through Christ Jesus.

8. Finally, brethren, whatsoever things are true, whatsoever things are honest, whatsoever things are just, whatsoever things are pure, whatsoever things are lovely, whatsoever things are of good report; if there be any virtue, and if there be any praise, think on these things.

Set Me Free

From every fear that grips my weary heart,
    From worries which distress and trouble me,
From every weight of doubt and anxious thoughts,
    Put forth Thy hand, oh Lord, and set me free.

From whispers of unhappy discontent,
    From all the stabbing pangs of jealousy,
From greed, uneasy and unsatisfied,
    Wilt Thou reach out, oh Lord, and set me free.

From bleak discouragement and downcast moods
    Which rob me of my usual energy,
Which settle like a great, dark cloud upon my heart,
    Reach through the gloom and set my spirit free.

From every bitter and malicious thought,
    From angry words which rise so hastily,
From deeds unkind and actions low and mean,
    Oh, God of Love, reach out and set me free.

From ugly pride which makes me want my way
    So badly that I act quite selfishly,
In disregard of others wants and plans,
    Oh, Lord, I pray, reach out and set me free.

And then I shall be free to trust Thee, Lord,
    To be content, to live most cheerfully,
To love my neighbor and to treat him well.
    How happy is the one Thou hast set free!

                -Mary E. Miller

by Becky Miller

When
Faith Points
the Way

--Mary Elaine Miller

Imagination can portray
　　With quick and skillful hand
The splendid things my self would choose
　　In terms I understand.
When Faith points out God's will for me,
　　How can Faith make me know
The blessings wonderful and great
　　My Father will bestow?
I am too inexperienced and
　　Too ignorant and small.
I could not grasp the worth of them
　　If I could see them all.
But I believe that as I tread
　　The way my Lord has planned,
My understanding shall increase,
　　My knowledge shall expand.
And many joys unthought of now
　　I know that I shall see
And revel in them when my Lord
　　Shall have His way with me.

The Artist

The brushes of diff'rent descriptions,
   The paints of the various hues,
The newly-hung canvas, still empty,
   Were ready for someone to use.
He came then, the talented artist.
   He patiently labored until
The beautiful picture was finished,
   A tribute to talent and skill.

But had it been done by another,
   A painter unlearned and untaught,
Though using the very same tools
   With which the great artist had wrought,
Would there have been found on the canvas
   Such evident beauty of art?
Ah, no, for the source of that beauty
   Is found in the talented heart.

And we, like the tools of the artist,
   Can boast of no skill of our own.
Ability, power, and talent
   Are found with the Master alone.
How wondrous the ways of God's working!
   No mortal can yet understand
How God can thus use any person
   Who trustfully rests in His hand.
And well may we rest, for His talent
   And wisdom and might are divine.
Oh, God, all the glory and honor
   For goodness and beauty are Thine!

--Mary Elaine Miller

283

Isaiah LXI

1. The Spirit of the Lord God is upon me; because the Lord hath anointed me to preach good tidings unto the meek; he hath sent me to bind up the brokenhearted, to proclaim liberty to the captives, and the opening of the prison to them that are bound;

2. To proclaim the acceptable year of the Lord, and the day of vengeance of our God; to comfort all that mourn;

3. To appoint unto them that mourn in Zion, to give unto them beauty for ashes, the oil of joy for mourning, the garment of praise for the spirit of heaviness; that they might be called trees of righteousness, the planting of the Lord, that he might be glorified.

Watching the Weaving

--Mary Elaine Miller

Before our eyes among the threads
   The busy shuttle flew.
A roll of cloth was being made.
   How steadily it grew!
The threads were strong. The weave was firm,
   The color, ivory,
With here and there a speck or two.
   These flaws were hard to see.
We thought the cloth most excellent,
   And we were pleased to scan
With friendly confidence and trust
   The making of a man.

An enemy came sneaking by;
   A ripping sound, a tear,
A gaping, jagged hole defaced
   The cloth beyond repair.
Large, ugly stains of inky black
   Made tracks across the white.
Before our eyes the cloth became
   A sorry, sorry sight.
How shocked we were! How grieved to find
   Our friend had been untrue
To his dear trust. We heard a voice,
   "Behold what sin can do!"

Then One came near. He held a cup
   Containing something red.
He freely spilled it on the stains.
   A length of shining thread
Began to close the ragged hole.
   He worked with patient care.
What love was in those tender eyes!
   What pity rested there!
We watched the needle flash about
   Hope flickered, stirred, and grew.
With bated breath we waited long
   To see what He could do.
At last He finished, stepped aside.
   The length of cloth unrolled.
The ugly rent had been repaired
   With silver threads and gold.
We thought the jagged tear had trailed
   A senseless, crooked line,
But now the darning threads had formed
   A meaningful design.

The once-black spots, now greatly changed
   To colors fair and bright,
In lovely patterns threw themselves
   Across the snowy white.

We clasped our hands in sudden joy,
   Amazed, inspired, and awed.
We saw no more the failing man
   For we beheld his God.

Who Am I?

Who am I
That a King should die
    In my place?
He offers me
Salvation free
    By His grace.

Who am I
That God on high
    Should hear each pray'r
And mark each tear
And hold me near
    Within His care?

Who am I
That great supply
    Of peace and love
Should fall on me
So graciously
    From God above?

Yes, undeserved,
Yet unreserved
    These gifts of His!
Behold the Lamb!
Not who I am,
    But who He is!

                --Mary E. Miller

Purity

The snow is fresh and pure and white
    When falling from the skies,
And like a blanket smooth and clean
    Upon the world it lies.

Lord, keep our minds as pure and clean
    As newly-fallen snow,
And when the sinful thoughts would come
    Then teach us where to go.

For if we look to Thee for aid,
    Such tempting thoughts must flee.
How pure and peaceful is Thy child
    Whose mind is stayed on Thee!

--Mary E. Miller

Hebrews XII

12. Wherefore lift up the hands which hang down, and the feeble knees;

13. And make straight paths for your feet, lest that which is lame be turned out of the way; but let it rather be healed.

14. Follow peace with all men, and holiness, without which no man shall see the Lord:

Without the Loss of One

E.R.M. & M.E.M.

E. Ruth and Mary E. Miller

1. With thank - ful - ness we praise Thee, Lord. What bless - ings Thou hast giv'n!
2. The loss of one— that tho't brings pain. How trag - ic that would be!
3. How beau - ti - ful that heav'n - ly home! The same word of com - mand

A bet - ter way of life on earth, A bet - ter home in heav'n.
Cease not to call, help us to guide The lost one un - to Thee.
That fash - ioned all the beau - ties here Has made the bet - ter land.

Chorus

So when our lives are fin - ished here, When our work here is done,

May Thou be pleased to call us home With - out the loss of one. A - MEN.

289

Early Snowdrops

Our Only Hope

--E. Ruth Miller

When life is good and hopes are high,
When love and sunshine fill the sky,
Our only hope must always be
In Christ who died for you and me.

When life is hard and love is lost,
When skies are dark and tempest tossed,
Our only hope we then will find
Is in the Saviour of mankind.

When life draws near its final day,
When sun shines forth its last, sweet ray,
Our only hope we then will know
Is in our God who loves us so.

Then look to Him and seek His way,
He who can cheer the darkest day,
That heav'n be ours when day is done.
This is our hope -- our only one.

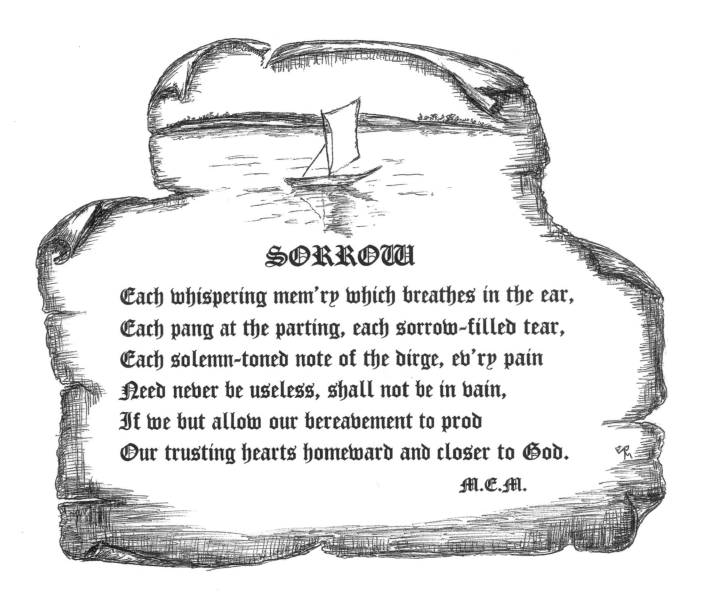

SORROW

Each whispering mem'ry which breathes in the ear,

Each pang at the parting, each sorrow-filled tear,

Each solemn-toned note of the dirge, ev'ry pain

Need never be useless, shall not be in vain,

If we but allow our bereavement to prod

Our trusting hearts homeward and closer to God.

M.E.M.

The Question

--Mary E. Miller

In eternity's golden and glorious reign
Will the once-mortal beings remember their pain?
If they do, will the phantom-like memories throw
Brief shadows of sorrow o'er heaven's bright glow?
   Will those memories trouble them still?

...Eye hath not seen, nor ear heard, neither have entered into the heart of man, the things which God hath prepared for them that love him.
I. Corinthians 2:9

The parents who watched as the agonized breath
Of their sunshine, their darling, was silenced by death;
Though the ache of their sorrow must quickly take flight
When they meet him again in the Land of Delight,
   Will the thought of that ache haunt them still?

And the city had no need of the sun, neither of the moon, to shine in it: for the glory of God did lighten it, and the Lamb is the light thereof.
Revelation 21:23

The woman whose blindness has plagued her from birth,
Who has seen not the manifold beauties of earth,
When her now-useless eyes the bright vision has caught
Of the glorious heavenly light, will the thought
   Of her handicap rankle her still?

The man who has longingly wished for a wife
To travel with him o'er the pathway of life;
When in heaven surrounded by infinite love
And perfect content, will the memory of
   His loneliness shadow him still?

The boy who has suffered from mockings and jeers
And thereby developed a complex of fears,
When he enters the city where only the word
Of gentle respectfulness ever is heard,
    Will the echo of scorn mock him still?

And God shall wipe away all tears from their eyes; and there shall be no more death, neither sorrow, nor crying, neither shall there be any more pain: for the former things are passed away. Revelation 21:4

The mother who knows that her days will be few,
Though she fears not to die, yet it grieves her anew
As she clasps her small child in a fervent embrace.
How painful to think of the grief he must face!
    In heav'n will that thought grieve her still?

...Hath not God chosen the poor of this world rich in faith, and heirs of the kingdom which he hath promised to them that love him? James 2:5

The couple whose struggles have only been met
By staggering losses and worrisome debt;
When heaven's own riches at last they possess,
Will the thought of their former financial distress
    Over shadow their ecstasy still?

Can he who has entered the city sublime
Remember to grieve over the sorrows of time?
When his tears have been dried by God's comforting touch,
Will the thought of the pain which had grieved him so much
    Continue to trouble him still?

When he sees that the pain which had wearied his heart
For many long years had played a great part
In drawing him unto the heavenly bliss;
Will there be any memory more cherished than this,
    To gladden and comfort him still?

Blessed are they that do his commandments, that they may have right to the tree of life, and may enter in through the gates into the city. Revelation 22:14

Lord, teach the discouraged disciples of Thine
    To trust in Thy infinite wisdom divine!
Throughout all the ages Thy wonderful ways
Shall be the glad objects of wonder and praise!
    Thy saints shall delight in them still.

II Timothy IV

6. For I am now ready to be offered, and the time of my departure is at hand.

7. I have fought a good fight, I have finished my course, I have kept the faith:

8. Henceforth there is laid up for me a crown of righteousness, which the Lord, the righteous judge, shall give me at that day: and not to me only, but unto all them also that love his appearing.

In Loving Memory of Vernon Miller

The Best Is Yet to Come

How can we let you go?
For we will miss you so
      While we remain.
To here no longer meet
Our circle incomplete
      What tears! What pain!

But let you go we will,
Though lonely days shall still
      Be wearisome.
In God's sweet will we rest
What calm! What joy! The best
      Is yet to come.   M.E.M.

My HOME by the River

by Mary Elaine Miller

A river in heaven--a wonderful thing!
It flows from the throne of our Father, the King.
Its life-giving waters eternally spring,
    The beautiful, heavenly river.

The Bride and the Spirit say, "Come." They invite
All those who are thirsty to turn to the right,
To trust in the Savior and drink with delight
    The water of life from the river.

And those who will hearken, and those who draw nigh
To drink of the water our God doth supply,
Who live for the Savior, will find by and by
    Their home in God's home by the river.

Once growing in Eden, the life-giving tree,
With twelve kinds of fruit, each a delicacy,
And leaves full of healing, abundant and free,
    Stands there on the bank of the river.

Do numberless little ones play by its side?
I know that in happiness there they abide,
No naughtiness causing a parent to chide
    To quiet their mirth by the river.

Our dear, faithful loved ones are joining the ranks
Of those who are walking the beautiful banks,
Delighting to render praise, glory, and thanks
    To Him Who sits there by the river.

God's radiant glory dispels thought of night.
He looks on His children with joyful delight.
He dries all their tears, and their troubles take flight,
    Up there by the beautiful river.

No sickness distresses, no weeds ever sprout.
Temptation and evil have all been cast out.
Nothing but goodness and gladness about
    In heaven, that home by the river.

I cannot imagine, much less can I tell,
The happiness felt by the spirits who dwell
Where sin cannot mar what our God doeth well
    In heaven, that home by the river.

When death at God's bidding shall call me away,
I'll part from my home at the end of life's day.
Delighted to be there, forever I'll stay
    In heaven, my HOME by the river.

*And the Spirit and the bride say, Come. And let him that heareth
say, Come. And let him that is athirst come. And whosoever will,
let him take the water of life freely. Revelation 22:17*

INDEX

POEMS

BIBLE VERSES

CHAPTER INTRODUCTIONS

EXCERPTS FROM THE DIARY AND CHRISTMAS LETTERS

HOW TO (Instructions)

PHOTOS

RECIPES